Presented To:

ROBERT

Date:

Kyle Mischel

Little Boys Bible Storybook

for Fathers and Sons

Little Boys Bible Storybook for Fathers & Sons

Text copyright © 2001 by Carolyn Larsen
Illustrations copyright © 2001 by Caron Turk

Scripture is taken from the *Holy Bible,* New Living
Translation, copyright © 1996. Used by permission of
Tyndale House Publishers, Inc., Wheaton, Illinois 60189. All
rights reserved.

New Kids Media™ is published by Baker Publishing Group,
Grand Rapids, Michigan.

ISBN 0-8010-4459-6

Third printing, June 2004

Printed in the United States of America

Little Boys Bible Storybook

for Fathers and Sons

Carolyn Larsen

Illustrated by Caron Turk

BAKER
A DIVISION OF
Baker Book House Co

Contents

Dear Dads,

The relationship a little boy has with his dad is so important. A good relationship helps establish a good self-image and self-confidence. Most little boys think their dads can do absolutely anything. Dad has a unique ability to teach his son the truths of the Bible and how to apply Scripture to life.

The Little Boys Bible Storybook for Fathers and Sons provides an opportunity to look at well-loved Bible stories through the eyes and hearts of the Bible characters who lived them. We don't really know how these people felt about the experiences they lived through. But, they were people like we are, so we can imagine how they felt. By thinking about how these people may have felt, we can learn lessons of how to apply Scripture to our lives and how to make God real in every aspect of life.

Caron Turk has once again hidden a little angel in each illustration. I know that you and your little boy will have fun looking for this little angel. Hopefully, you'll be able to discuss the Bible story as you do your angel search. Caron and I pray that this book will provide hours of "together time" and entertainment with a purpose for you and your son. We pray that you will grow closer together and that both you and your son will go deeper in your relationship with the Lord through reading and talking about this book.

God bless,

Carolyn Larsen

How It All Began

"You're a bear. You look like a . . . rabbit. Hmm, I'll call you a turtle," Adam took the job of naming the animals very seriously. God was trusting him to do a good job. "Wow, you sure made a lot of animals, God. How did you think of so many different kinds?" Adam asked, taking a break. Thinking up names was hard work.

"I'm glad you asked. Let me tell you how this world came to be," God answered.

"In the beginning, not a star twinkled, not a bird sang, not a bug crawled. Everything was dark and quiet and empty," God said.

"Sounds kind of boring," Adam whispered.

"Exactly. So I said, 'Let there be light!' and light exploded into the darkness. I made day and night and earth and sky. Then I filled the land with every kind of plant I could think of . . . trees, bushes, flowers, grass and . . ."

"That must have taken a long time," Adam interrupted.

"Not really, that took only three days."

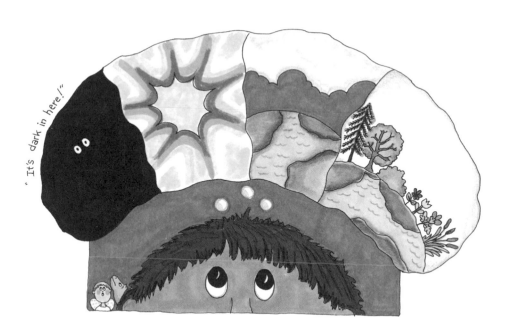

"Three days, wow," Adam was amazed. "What did you do next?"

"The fourth day is one of my favorites," God smiled. "I sprinkled stars in the night sky, made the bright sun to light the day, and the gentle moon to light the night."

"All that in one day? You were certainly busy!" Adam was impressed.

"The fifth day I noticed how empty the oceans were . . . so I filled them with fish and dolphins, octopus and eels, all kinds of things that swim."

"It must have been fun to think of all those things," Adam said. "I like to watch dolphins jumping out of the water. When did you make the birds?"

"On that very same day. From big bald eagles to tiny humming birds, I filled the sky with all kinds of things that fly."

"The sixth day started off with animals. Big lions, soft rabbits . . . any animal I could think of. When I finished making animals, I turned my attention to you," God continued.

"Me?" Adam didn't know what to think.

"Yes, I made you, Adam, to be able to think and make decisions. You can love and care for others. You are a lot like me."

"Wow, that's awesome. What did you do next?" Adam wondered.

"I looked around at all I had made and I liked everything I saw. I knew I had done my very best. So, on the seventh day, I took a rest," God said.

Based on Genesis 1

Becoming a Man of God
A man of God is made in God's image.

God had some wonderful ideas, didn't he? He thought of all kinds of unusual animals—some are funny looking and some are kind of scary. He even made animals that make nice pets for us. He also thought of all kinds of flowers with hundreds of different colors and scents.

But, God's best creation . . . the one he saved for last . . . was people! He made people to be a lot like him. We can think and make decisions and learn the difference between the right and wrong. He even gave that first person a job to do. He trusted Adam to name all the animals and he asked Adam and Eve to take care of the Garden of Eden.

You are made in God's image, too. He made you the way you are . . . with a kind heart and jolly laugh. He gave you interests in sports or science or carpentry, or whatever you like to do. Be happy with who you are! Learn more about the interests and talents that God gave you and how you can use them to help other people.

Dad's Turn

Share with your son a memory about things you liked
to do when you were a little boy. Did you enjoy
fishing with your dad or helping your grandfather
build things? Maybe you loved making cookies with
your mom. Does he have any of the same interests
that you had as a child?

It's so important for your son to know how proud you
are of him. Point out things about him that you
appreciate . . . his kindness, sense of humor,
helpfulness. Then remind him of the activities you
and he enjoy doing together. Tell him how special he
is to you . . . and to God!

A Verse to Remember

God created people in his own image; God patterned
them after himself; male and female he created them.
Genesis 1:27

The Bite That Changed the World

"Eve, what do you think you're doing?" Adam shouted. "You heard the rules the same as I did. It wasn't difficult. God said, 'Everything in the garden is for you. Eat what you want, pick the flowers you want. But, don't touch the tree in the middle of the garden.' Now, you're holding fruit from that tree . . . with a bite out of it! You're in big trouble!"

"Adam, relax, God didn't mean all that the way we took it. That lovely snake there explained it to me," Eve waved the fruit around as she spoke.

Adam just shook his head and walked away, but Eve chased him through the garden. "The snake pointed out that if we ate fruit from that particular tree, we would actually be more like God. Look at me. I tasted it and I didn't drop dead, did I? Come on, give it a try," Eve begged.

But Adam ignored her and went over to a stream. He dragged a reed through the water and tried to pretend none of this was happening.

Eve wasn't going to let this go. "Come on. This is the sweetest, juiciest fruit you'll ever taste. I'm telling you, you'll thank me after you taste it." She waved the fruit under his nose. He could smell it's sweetness and see the juice running through her fingers and dripping on the ground. Suddenly, Adam grabbed it out of her hand and sunk his teeth into the soft red skin. "Yumm, this IS delicious," he mumbled, as juice dripped down his chin.

Adam slurped in the last little bit of juice, and, out of the corner of his eye he saw the snake slither away. It seemed to be smiling. "Oh no, Eve, do you know what we've done?" Adam cried. Tears rolled down his cheeks, "God gave us one simple rule and the freedom to enjoy everything else he made, but we broke that one rule. We disobeyed God."

Later that day, God came to visit with Adam and Eve . . . but he couldn't find them. They were hiding because they were so ashamed. Right away, God knew what had happened. "Oh, Adam. I know what you have done and I'm so sad that you disobeyed me. It means I have to punish you. You'll have to leave the garden and find a new place to live and grow your own food to eat. But, always remember this-just because I punish you doesn't mean I don't love you. I will always, always love you."

Based on Genesis 3

The Lord God sent Adam and Eve from the garden...

Becoming a Man of God

A man of God knows God loves him, no matter what.

Adam and Eve were made in God's image. That means that they could think and make decisions and choices . . . and they made a bad one. They chose to do what the tricky snake said instead of obeying the one rule that God gave them. They disobeyed and that meant God had to punish them. Why? Well, disobedience means punishment because otherwise, we just keep right on disobeying-even doing things that are bad for us. Rules are generally made to protect us. But, the important thing to remember is that God didn't stop loving Adam and Eve when they sinned. He was sad and probably disappointed in their choice, but he didn't stop loving them.

Since Adam and Eve sinned, everybody sins. No matter how hard we try, we can never be perfect. But, when we sin, we can ask God to forgive us and he will! He loves us, no matter what!

Dad's Turn

OK Dad, it's time to come clean. Let your son know that you sometimes make mistakes, even as an adult. First, tell him about a time when as a child you disobeyed your parents or caregivers. What was the situation? Were you punished? Share with him ways that adults have problems with disobedience, for example, obeying the speed limit.

You may be able to remind your son of a recent incident when he disobeyed. Reinforce that even though you didn't like his actions, you still love him very much. Remind him that everyone sins. We all disobey or do unkind things sometimes. But, God will always forgive our sins, if we ask him. Tell your son that God loves him and so do you!

A Verse to Remember
Nothing can ever separate us from his love.
Romans 8:38

Losing Control

"Sissy, sissy, Abel is a sissy!" Cain sang, dancing around his brother, picking up a lamb and waving it in the air. "Do you want to spend the rest of your life following dumb sheep around? Why don't you get a real job?"

"Cain, grow up. Just because you like being a farmer doesn't mean I have to. Why do you have to make fun of everything I do?" Some days Abel couldn't stand his older brother. He was always picking a fight about something.

One morning Cain was working in a field near where Abel's sheep were eating breakfast. Abel didn't notice Cain watching him build a little altar of stones. He concentrated on giving his offering to God. Abel loved God and tried to live the way God wanted.

"Look at that," Cain moaned. "If he's giving an offering to God, I guess I have to give one, too. He makes me so mad! He's such a goody-two-shoes!"

Cain pulled some scraggly grain from his field . . . not the
best he had, by any means. He made a half-hearted offering,
then went on with his work. But, to his surprise, God refused
his offering! Even worse, God accepted Abel's offering! "THIS
ISN'T FAIR!!" Cain screamed so loud that Abel's sheep ran to
hide.

   "Cain, calm down," God whispered. "Make your
offering in the right way, with the right attitude in your heart
and I'll accept it. Be careful of that jealousy boiling in your
heart."

But Cain didn't pay any attention to God's warning. His anger built up to a monster level that he couldn't control. He came up with an ugly, evil plan. "Yoohoo, Abel, my wonderful brother," he said sweetly. "Would you help with something out in my field?"

"Sure, anything," Abel said, following Cain into the field. Suddenly, Cain swung a big log around and smacked Abel in the head. Abel's face looked completely surprised as he fell to the ground—dead.

"Take that you lousy do-gooder," Cain thought as he jogged
back home. "No one saw me kill Abel. I'm home free."

But then, God's voice rang through the stillness,
"Where is your brother, Abel?"

"Hey, it's not my day to watch him!" Cain snapped
sarcastically.

"Abel's blood cries out from the ground. You
murdered him, Cain. You must leave here and wander
around with no home for the rest of your life!" God ordered.

Based on Genesis 4:1-12

Becoming a Man of God

A man of God gives God the best he has.

Cain didn't really care about God. If he did, he would have worshiped God whether Abel did or not. Also, when he did make an offering to God, he would have given the very best of what he had, not left-overs or grain that he would have thrown away.

But, you know, Cain could have given good grain, and he could have made an offering every day and that would have looked good to anyone who was watching. But, God looks at the heart and he would have been able to tell that Cain's heart wasn't worshiping God. Everything Cain did was for show, not for worship.

How do you worship God? Do you sing, pray, read the Bible? How can you give him the best of what you have?

Dad's Turn

Worshiping God is a privilege and a responsibility. The way you worship God will have a big influence on your son. He may observe you going to church each week, or attending Bible study, even saying grace before dinner. But, is it obvious that your heart is worshiping God by the way you speak about church leaders or the way you treat other people?

Talk with your son about having the right attitude of worship in your heart. Explain to him what worship means to you. Talk about ways you give God your best, through your money, time and talents. Help your son plan ways that he can give God his best. Pray together about having the right heart attitude of worship.

A Verse to Remember

Give honor to the LORD for the glory of his name. Worship the LORD in the splendor of his holiness.
Psalm 29:2

Water Works

"Your feet stink, get them out of my face!" Japheth shouted.

"Oh yeah, well your breath stinks, don't breathe on my feet!" Ham shouted back at his little brother.

"Be quiet!" Shem moaned. "Every bone in my body aches and you two just interrupted my last few minutes of sleep! I know it's a good thing that Dad is building the big boat, but it sure is hard work."

After the three brothers finished breakfast they went out to help their dad. He was building a boat, the biggest boat anyone had ever seen. God told him to build it because a great-big-earth-cleaning flood was coming. God was tired of the way people lived—only thinking about themselves—evil and selfish and paying no attention to God. Everyone except their dad, Noah. He obeyed God, that's why God warned him about the flood.

When the boat was finished, the boys happily went back to their old chores, which seemed pretty easy now. One day Japheth was playing outside when he noticed something strange, "Dad, zillions of animals are marching straight toward the boat!"

Noah smiled, "God is sending two of every kind of animal to go in the boat. He wants them to be safe, too. Then, after the flood, they will have babies so there will be animals on earth again."

A few days later Noah cried, "Grab your carry-ons, boys, it's time to get in the boat." Soon they heard raindrops pounding on the roof. It rained so long that the whole earth flooded. All the people died . . . except the Noah family, safe inside the boat. One morning, forty days after the first raindrop fell, Shem shushed his noisy brothers, "Listen!" But they didn't hear anything. "I know . . . it's quiet! The rain has finally stopped! Yahoo!" the brothers cheered because their stinky boat ride (after all, it was full of animals!) would soon be over.

"Calm down," Noah smiled. "God will tell us when to leave. There's still lots of water out there." At least once a day someone asked, "Is it time yet?" Finally, one day they all came out of the boat to a clean new world.

Noah called everyone together, "See that rainbow in the sky? That shows God's promise to us that he will never send such a big flood again. Let's take time to thank him." Then the whole family (and maybe a few smart animals) knelt and thanked God for his love and protection.

Based on Genesis 6-9

Becoming a Man of God
A man of God obeys God.

The Noah boys grew up in a family that loved and honored God. The whole family probably took some heavy teasing from friends and neighbors when their dad started building the big boat. But, the boys knew that their father would always choose to obey God, even when that wasn't the easy or popular thing to do. Since he did obey, the Noah family were the only people left on earth after the big flood. The first thing Noah led his family to do after they got off the smelly boat was to take time to thank God for his love and protection.

You know that the right thing to do is obey God, obey your parents, obey teachers. But sometimes, that isn't the easy thing to do. When was a time that you obeyed and you were glad you did? When was a time when you didn't obey and you were later sorry?

Dad's Turn

When you're a kid sometimes it seems like someone is
always telling you what to do. Obeying can get pretty
old. Tell your son about a time when you obeyed, even
though it was difficult. Were you later glad you obeyed?
Now, tell him about a time when you didn't obey,
because it was hard to or because your friends wanted
you to do something different. Were you sorry you
disobeyed? What happened?

Obeying God can be extra hard if your friends don't care
anything about him. Encourage your son to do the right
thing even if his friends want him to do something else.
Remind him to always obey . . . and to remember to
thank God for his love and care.

A Verse to Remember
Those who obey God's word really do love him.
1 John 2:5

Huh? What Did You Say?

There once was a time when every person on earth spoke the same language. No matter where a person went he could ask, "How do I get to the store?" or, "How are your kids doing?" It was wonderful! Everyone could talk to everyone else. But then . . .

"Hey, you guys. I've got a super idea! Why don't we build a new city? Look, I've already drawn up some plans. It will be the biggest, most beautiful city ever." People hurried to look at the drawings and everyone agreed to work together and build a city that would be better than anything else ever built.

The people got right to work. Some made bricks and others stacked the bricks into walls. Some dug holes to be the foundations of the buildings. It was hard work! One day someone said, "What our city needs is a big, big tower . . . so high that it reaches the sky! Then everyone in the rest of the world will know how smart and powerful we are."

THE TOWER

But, the smart and powerful people forgot all about God! He was sad to hear the way they were talking. They thought they were so smart and powerful that they didn't even need him anymore. "They think they are so great, but they are leaving me completely out," God said. "How can I get their attention again?" Then, God came up with a plan.

The next morning one workman said, "Toss me that brick!"
But, his buddies couldn't understand him! "Huh? What did he
say?" someone asked . . . but no one could understand that
man either! Everyone was speaking different languages!
People quickly looked around for people they could
understand. Pretty soon everyone divided into groups with
people who spoke the same way. The big tower and the fancy
city were completely forgotten . . . but God wasn't!

Based on Genesis 11:1-9

Becoming a Man of God
A man of God glorifies God, not himself.

What were these guys thinking? This group of men got so caught up in their fancy building that they completely forgot about God. They didn't think they even needed him anymore. Their grand ideas and fancy tower made them think they were very clever and important. They were shouting to the world, "Hurrah for me!" instead of "Hurrah for God!"

God took care of that attitude, didn't he? He knew that if they couldn't understand each other or communicate with each other, they wouldn't be able to work together on the tower. So, he created new languages. God wants people to realize they need him and to remember to give him the glory for whatever gifts and talents he gives them.

What kinds of things are you good at doing? Sports? Music? Reading? When you do those things do you enjoy having people tell you how great you are? Do you remember to thank God for those talents and gifts? Remember to glorify him in everything you do.

Dad's Turn

The men who built the Tower of Babel were pretty creative, weren't they? They were also pretty ambitious. What is the biggest, most challenging thing you've ever tackled? The problem with the people in the story was that they decided they didn't need God. They thought they could do something (build a big tower) that would make them powerful and important. They were glorifying themselves instead of God. Give your son an example of how to glorify God. What are the talents or gifts God has given you? How do you use those for God's glory?

Talk with your son about how important it is to glorify God by what we do . . . not ourselves. Suggest things you could do together on a daily basis—read a Bible story, pray together, talk about things God does for you every day. Suggest that your son can glorify God by the way he plays with his siblings, or treats God's creation. What are some other ways?

A Verse to Remember

Let us continually offer our sacrifice of praise to God by proclaiming the glory of his name.

Hebrews 13:15

Who's Number one?

"A baby. I can't believe we have a baby. I'm so old that my knees crack every time I bend down, but I have a baby. It's a miracle. God is so good to us," Sarah couldn't stop looking at baby Isaac. She and Abraham had wanted a baby for a long, long time, and God had finally given them a son. Abraham was right beside her, staring in amazement at his son.

As Isaac grew up, Abraham taught him things he would need
to know as he grew into manhood. "Isaac, the most important
thing I can teach you is to honor God in all you do. I want
you to come with me to give a sacrifice to God," Abraham
sounded a little strange as he spoke these words. But, Isaac
didn't even notice because he was so excited to be included
in this special time. He had seen his dad go into the
mountains many times to make an offering to God.

Isaac ran ahead of his dad, picking up stones and flinging them high in the air. Running back to Abraham, he asked the question that had been hanging around in the back of his mind, "How come you didn't bring a lamb to sacrifice like you usually do?"

Abraham took a deep breath before answering, "God will provide the sacrifice, my son."

God will provide, my son

Isaac wasn't exactly sure what his dad meant . . . until they reached the top of the mountain. "My precious son, you are the sacrifice." Tears rolled down Abraham's cheeks as he prepared to sacrifice his own son.

Just as his shaking arm raised the knife a voice said, "Stop, Abraham. Don't hurt your son. You have shown that you love God more than anything, and that's the way it should be."

Isaac breathed a sigh of relief when his dad untied him.
Abraham hugged him so hard that Isaac thought his ribs
were going to crack. Together they sacrificed a ram that God
provided. Then they praised God, who would one day
sacrifice his only Son for people he loved so very much.

Based on Genesis 22

Becoming a Man of God
A man of God loves God most of all.

Wow! Isaac learned a powerful lesson from his dad, didn't he? Abraham lived an excellent example of loving God most of all. Now, there's no doubt that Abraham loved his son very much. But, he loved God more . . . and trusted God completely. Abraham knew that nothing and no one should be more important to him than God. He also knew that God loved him and Isaac and he trusted God to do what was best for both of them.

Who is important to you? Name the people that you love the most. Is it hard to make sure that God is more important to you than those people? Take time right now to thank God for putting those people in your life.

Dad's Turn

Tell your son how very important he is to you. Tell him about the day he was born and how you felt. Talk about the thoughts that ran through your mind the first time you held him in your arms.

Share a time when you struggled with something or someone becoming too important in your life. Was it a job, sport, person? How did you come to realize that this thing or person had become more important than God? How did you handle it?

Discuss with your son the things or people that are important to him. Reinforce that it is good to care about people and things, but that those things should never be more important than God. He should always have first place in our hearts.

A Verse to Remember

You must love the LORD your God with all your heart, all your soul, and all your strength.

Deuteronomy 6:5

Good News . . . Bad News

"So, how do you like it down there? You can stay there 'til you rot . . . don't feel so special now, do you?" Joseph's brothers were fed up with him. "Dad likes you best and he doesn't even try to hide it. He gives you fancy presents, like this coat, but does he ever have anything for us? Of course not! Then you have these unbelievable dreams that we're going to bow down to you—you're going to rule over us! Get over yourself, brother!"

Joseph's brothers were actually going to let him die in that hole! Just when he thought it was hopeless, Joseph heard them whispering to each other. Maybe they had changed their minds! "Yeah, I see them . . . slave traders, probably on the way to Egypt," he heard. "Not a bad idea. Yeah, I like it. We sell them the kid—tell Dad an animal killed him. He's out of our hair and we won't be guilty of murder. Best of all, Mr. 'I'm-so-important' will be a slave! Haa haaa haaa!" Joseph didn't like the way this was going.

"The bad news is, I'm a slave. The good news is Potiphar liked me and put me in charge of his house. The bad news is, Mrs. Potiphar lied about me so now I'm in jail," Joseph had plenty of time to think about his situation. "Well, I'm going to keep on trusting God to take care of me. He hasn't let me down yet, so I'll keep praying to him, every day!"

"Are you feeling ill today, Sir?" Pharaoh's advisor asked.

"Not really, but I had nightmares last night and I couldn't sleep. I remember them, but I can't figure out what they meant," the Egyptian king answered.

"Sir, I've heard there is a young man in our prison who can explain dreams," the servant said.

Before he finished speaking, Pharaoh shouted, "Get him!" God helped Joseph explain the Pharaoh's dreams. He was so happy that he made Joseph the second highest commander of the country!

A little while later, there was a terrible drought—no food would grow anywhere. But, God had warned Joseph about it and he stored up lots of food. People even came from other countries to buy some. One day, Joseph saw some men waiting to buy food. They didn't recognize him, but Joseph knew who they were! His own brothers—the ones who had sold him into slavery. He could have thrown them in jail, or even had them killed. But, he didn't. "Hey brothers, it's me, Joseph. I forgive you for trying to hurt me. I'm so glad to see you." That's exactly what God wanted Joseph to do!

Based on Genesis 37-45

Becoming a Man of God
A man of God forgives others.

If anyone ever had a reason to be mad at someone, it was Joseph. His brothers did a very mean and spiteful thing to him. God took the things they meant to be bad and turned them into good for Joseph, because Joseph loved and trusted God.

Then when his brothers really needed to buy food from him, Joseph had a perfect opportunity for revenge. What a great chance to get even . . . but he didn't. Once again, the important thing to remember is that Joseph loved God and he knew that the right thing to do would be to forgive his brothers. That's what he did, and he showed a wonderful example of how God forgives his children for the wrong things we do.

Have you ever been really angry with someone who was mean to you? What did they do to you? Did you do something back to them? How did you feel afterward?

Dad's Turn

Share a memory with your son of a time when someone did something mean to you. How did you respond to that person? Did you get even with him or her? Now recall a time when you forgave someone's actions toward you instead of taking revenge.

This could come down to a discussion of what is "macho" versus what is godly. Teach your son that it isn't wimpy to forgive someone instead of getting even with them. In fact, it takes a bigger person to forgive without getting even.

Thank God together for this story that is an example of his forgiveness. Thank him for forgiving our sinful actions.

A Verse to Remember

Love your enemies. Pray for those who persecute you.
Matthew 5:44

Mom's Good Plan

"No! Pharaoh and his creepy soldiers can't have my precious baby!" Jochebed stomped around the room holding the baby so tightly that a loud b-u-r-pppp popped from his lips.

"Honey, I love this baby as much as you, but Pharaoh ordered that all Hebrew baby boys be killed. We're just two lowly slaves, how are we going to stop it?" her husband asked in frustration.

Jochebed had already been thinking about how to save her son. A few days later she put her plan into action. "Miriam, hold your brother and try to keep him quiet," she ordered. Miriam watched in confusion as her mom raced out of the house. She returned a while later carrying an armload of reeds. Quickly, Jochebed wove the reeds into a little basket with a lid. Miriam couldn't figure out what her mom was planning to do.

"Come on, we're going down to the river," Jochebed announced, when the basket was finished. They slipped through back streets, hiding behind trees when they saw another person. When they reached the river, Jochebed said, "Give me the baby." She gently laid her little boy in the basket. Giving him one last kiss, she put the cover on and shoved the basket onto the water. "What happens to him now is in God's hands," she whispered.

Tears streamed down Jochebed's face while she walked home. Miriam hid at the edge of the river and watched her little brother's basket float away. It was moving close to where the Egyptian princess often came to bathe in the river. Sure enough, a few minutes later Miriam heard the laughter of the princess and her servants. "What if she sees the basket? Will she give the baby to her father? Will my brother be killed after all?" Miriam's heart pounded so hard that she was afraid the princess would hear it.

The princess spotted the basket immediately. "Bring it to me," she ordered. When they took the cover off, Miriam could hear her brother crying. "A Hebrew baby. Isn't he cute? I want to keep him," the princess announced.

Miriam bounded out of the grass before she could think about what she was doing. "Your highness, would you like a Hebrew woman to be his nurse?" The princess said yes and Miriam dashed home, "Momma, come quick. The princess is going to keep the baby and she wants someone take care of him!"

Based on Exodus 2:1-10

Becoming a Man of God

A man of God does what he can.

Jochebed could have just thrown her hands up in despair and said, "Oh well, I guess Pharaoh will kill my son." But, Jochebed wasn't like that. She loved her baby boy very much and she was willing to do whatever she could to keep him alive. She used her brain to think up a plan and she used the talents God gave her to make the basket. God blessed her efforts and the little baby's life was saved.

There are times when the best thing we can do is pray and trust God with how a situation will turn out. But, there are also times when we should use our brains and the abilities God has given us to solve our problems. So when we have a problem to solve or a project to do we should pray for guidance and help, then . . . get busy!

When was a time you thought through how to solve a problem, then did it?

Dad's Turn

Give your son two examples-one of a situation where you came up with a plan to solve a problem, then put the plan into action. Perhaps, this example would be of a larger situation, where you were part of a large group working to solve the problem. Next, give him an example of a situation where your hands were tied, and all you could do was pray and trust God with the solution. Tell him how both situations turned out.

Ask your son if there are any situations he is currently concerned about, such as homeless people in your city, or a friend at school who is having a hard time. Come up with a plan together for something you can do to help, then work on it together.

A Verse to Remember
Think of ways to encourage one another to outbursts of love and good deeds.
Hebrews 10:24

A True Sign

Moses was shaking in his sandals . . . well, he would have been if he were wearing sandals! In fact, he wanted to turn and run as far away from the burning bush as he could. But, God was in that bush (that's why it was burning) and Moses knew he couldn't run away from God.

"Moses, you're going to free my people from slavery," God announced. "Tell the Israelites that I've put you in charge. Then, go to the Pharaoh of Egypt and tell him that I said to let my people go!"

"You've got the wrong guy," Moses whispered. "I'm just a shepherd. I take care of sheep, not people. Who would listen to me? Why would anyone believe that you put me in charge?" He was backing away from the bush a step at a time now.

"What have you got in your hand?" God asked.

"Why does he all of a sudden care about my equipment?

Moses wondered. "It's just my shepherd staff," he answered, holding it up for God to see.

"Throw it down on the ground," God said.

"What?"

"Throw it down," God said again. Moses tossed the staff in front of the bush.

Suddenly, it scooted right back at Moses . . . it had turned
into a snake! Moses screamed and backed up so fast that he
fell right down (if there was one thing he didn't like, it was
snakes). "Pick it up by the tail," God ordered. Moses looked at
the hissing snake. Then at the burning bush . . . snake . . .
bush. Closing his eyes, he grabbed the snake's tail. Instantly,
it was his staff again! It sort of sounded like God was smiling
as he said, "Do this for the Israelites, then they will believe I
sent you."

Based on Exodus 3:1-4:5

Becoming a Man of God
A man of God takes a chance.

God had a lot of trust in Moses. He asks Moses to do a very big job . . . and God knew it wasn't going to be easy. Moses' job was taking care of sheep. He probably thought he would be a shepherd for the rest of his life. But, God had bigger plans. However, when God shared those plans with Moses, instead of leaping at the chance, Moses was scared! Being scared was OK, because God was asking him to do something new and something big. He should have been scared—but he should have also trusted God for help.

Moses took a little convincing, and God knew that the stick-to-snake thing would do the trick. So, it took Moses a little time, and he needed the help of a little miracle, to realize that this was GOD talking to him. When he understood that, Moses left his sheep and took a chance. He obeyed God's request and trusted God to help him.

Have you ever been a little scared at something new you had to do? How did you get over being afraid?

Dad's Turn

Your son may look at you and think that you are never, ever afraid of anything. While that may make you feel cool, it would help him to know that sometimes you are afraid or nervous about things. Share a time when you have been afraid, especially of something new. Perhaps it was a time from your childhood when your family moved to a new town and you had to attend a new school. Maybe it was a big project at work that looked overwhelming to you. Or, maybe it was something you knew that God was asking you to do—go on a missions trip, or serve on a committee or board.

Explain how the situation turned out and what part your faith played in the outcome. Did you sense God's presence through this experience?

Ask your son if there are things in his life that frighten him? Are there things that he thinks could or might happen in the future that make him nervous. Remind him of the ways God has shown his presence to your family in the past and that these experiences show you can trust him for the future.

A Verse to Remember

My help comes from the LORD, who made the heavens
and the earth!
Psalm 121:2

"Let My People Go!"

"Why did you come here? You've caused nothing but trouble. Asking Pharaoh to let us go made him mad. So now, he's made us work even harder! Why can't you just be quiet?" The angry people let Moses have it with both barrels! Moses just shook his head-he was only doing what God told him to do-and God had to talk him into it in the first place!

"God," Moses prayed, "you're going to have to do something to show the Israelites and Pharaoh that you mean business!" Well, that was certainly no problem because God had a plan . . . all the water in Egypt turned to blood! Egyptians could be heard shouting, "What will we drink? The fish are all dead! Yuck, it smells!" But did this miracle make Pharaoh let the Israelites leave? Not on your life!

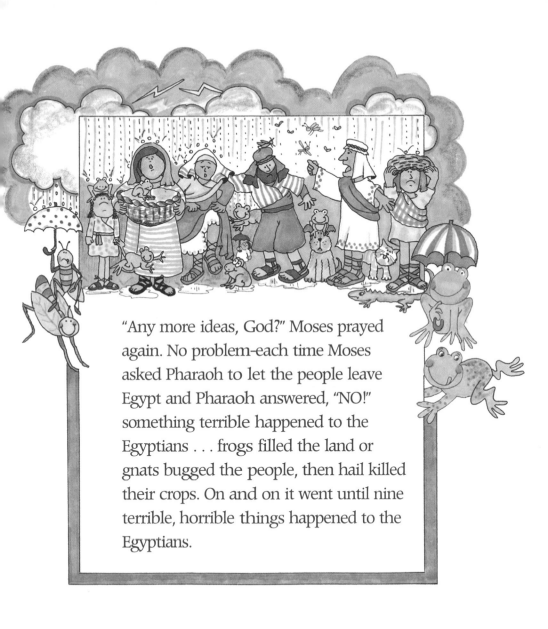

"Any more ideas, God?" Moses prayed again. No problem-each time Moses asked Pharaoh to let the people leave Egypt and Pharaoh answered, "NO!" something terrible happened to the Egyptians . . . frogs filled the land or gnats bugged the people, then hail killed their crops. On and on it went until nine terrible, horrible things happened to the Egyptians.

Each time some new plague hit, Pharaoh called Moses back to the palace and said, "OK, OK, OK, stop this plague and I'll let you take the people out of Egypt." But, every time God called off the plague, Pharaoh changed his mind again. Finally, after the ninth plague, the Egyptian people were getting sick of this. "Maybe Pharaoh should just let them go!" some Egyptians whispered to each other at the town well.

Meanwhile, the Israelites were discouraged and Moses was confused. "Didn't God say he was going to deliver us from Egypt? Why hasn't Pharaoh let us leave?" Moses did the only thing he could think of. He knelt down and poured out his heart to God, "Are my people going to die here? Are we going to always be slaves? O God, what's going on? Have you forgotten us?"

Of course, God had a plan. One more terrible, horrible thing would happen that would convince Pharaoh once and for all to let the Israelites go.

Based on Exodus 7:1-10:29

Becoming a Man of God
A man of God goes to God with his problems.

Remember when God talked to Moses at the burning bush? He asked Moses to lead his people out of Egypt, so Moses knew that he was doing a job God had given him to do. So, why was it so hard? Moses may have wondered why the Pharaoh didn't just say, "Oh, you want to take the Israelites out of Egypt, OK, go ahead." After all, the whole thing was God's idea. But, just because a job comes from God doesn't mean it's going to be easy. Besides, not everyone cares what God says about things (Pharaoh, for example).

So, when the going got tough, Moses did the best thing he could possibly do-he talked to God about the problem. He told God how frustrated he was about the situation. He asked God what to do next, and he reminded God that he was trusting him for help.

What do you do when you have a problem? Who do you talk to about it? Has there been a time when you've prayed about a problem and then knew for sure that God helped you with it?

Dad's Turn

Your son will learn a lot about how to handle problems and difficulties by watching how you handle them. Does he know that you take your problems to God? What's the biggest problem or most difficult situation you remember facing as a child? Why was it so difficult? How did you handle it? Did you pray about it?

Can you share a time when you prayed diligently about something, and saw God's hand in the solution? Did that make it easier to trust God the next time you had a problem? Remind your son that remembering how God has worked in the past makes it easier to trust him the next time. Remind him too, that when God gives you a job to do, he will always help you do it.

A Verse to Remember

God will surely do this for you, for he always does just what he says.

1 Corinthians 1:9

Follow that Cloud!

God had one more terrible, horrible miracle in mind to convince Pharaoh to let the Israelites leave Egypt. The firstborn son in every Egyptian home died—even Pharaoh's son. After that, Pharaoh turned to Moses and through his tears he whispered, "Get out of Egypt!"

God came in a huge cloud and led the people out of Egypt. At night the cloud turned to fire. The Israelites knew that God was leading them.

"We'll camp here," Moses announced when they were near the Red Sea. Women made dinner as their children ran and played.

Things were fine until someone shouted, "What's that cloud of dust over there?"

"It's Pharaoh's army! He's changed his mind again and sent his soldiers to bring us back." In a split second the Israelites were all over Moses again, "Did you bring us out here to die? We should have stayed in Egypt!" What would Moses do now?

"Watch what God will do for you!" Moses shouted, climbing up on a rock. He held his big shepherd's staff out over the water and a strong wind began to blow. The water of the Red Sea splashed and blew. The people squished together as they backed away from the sea. Mumbles of, "What's going on? What is he doing?" rolled through the crowd.

"God is saving you," Moses cried. The wind blew harder and harder, finally blowing the water into two big walls. The ground between the walls was . . . dry. There wasn't even a drop of mud.

"What does this mean?" the people wondered, staring at the water hallway.

"Go on through!" Moses cried. The frightened people held back until one man finally stepped out. The people followed him, eyeing the big water walls with wonder.

It took a long time for all the people to cross through the sea, even though they hurried as fast as they could. "The Egyptian army is following us into the sea," the Israelites screamed.

"Hurry through," Moses called to the last few people. Then he raised his hand over the sea again, and the water crashed over the soldiers and chariots. Every Egyptian soldier died in the Red Sea that day, but God kept every Israelite safe!

Based on Exodus 14

Becoming a Man of God
A man of God sticks with a job.

Remember w-a-a-a-y back when God talked to Moses at the burning bush? That's when God told Moses to free the Israelites from slavery in Egypt. Remember how after Moses got to Egypt, the pharaoh wouldn't let the people go? And the people complained about Moses getting them in trouble with the pharaoh? Well, there may have been times when Moses wanted to give up and leave the people to their complaining, but he didn't. Moses stuck with the job God had given him. Moses decided to finish the job, and he didn't let problems and complaining stop him.

It's important to keep in mind that every time Moses or the people had a problem, every step of the way, Moses talked to God. He asked God's help and waited for God's leading. God and Moses were a great team!

Have you ever had a job to do that seemed too big for you? Maybe you had to clean your messy room, or maybe you had tons of homework, or perhaps you were supposed to help Dad rake leaves in the yard. Did you stick with the job until it was finished? Was it hard to do that?

Dad's Turn

Two lessons grow from this story—a good work ethic and dependence on God. Your son will learn a good work ethic by watching how you approach work. Children watch their parents, even when it doesn't seem like they are paying any attention, and both of these examples will be noticed. Share a story with your son of a job you faced that seemed completely overwhelming. Tell him if you were tempted to quit before the job was finished. Tell him how you felt when the job was finished.

When was a time that you truly trusted God for help with a situation? How did God help you through this situation? Ask your son if he has anything facing him that seems overwhelming. Pray with him about the big job. Then, see if you can work out a schedule to help him take the job in small chunks and work through the entire situation.

A Verse to Remember

Those who wait on the LORD will find new strength. They will fly high on wings like eagles. They will run and not grow weary. They will walk and not faint.

Isaiah 40:31

Hard Water

Moses dug his shepherd's staff into the sand and pulled himself up the small hill. "I'm so tired, but I can't stop," he thought. "God gave me the job of leading the Israelites out of Egypt and time after time God has done miracles so the people would know that he's with us. Now thousands and thousands of men, women and children are depending on me. I have to keep going."

"Wow, it's hot out here," someone said. "Yeah, the sun is beating down," someone else added. Pretty soon, everyone around Moses was complaining about the heat. "Why can't we stop and get a drink?" someone shouted from a few rows back. "A DRINK? Do you SEE any water around here?" the first man shouted back.

"We're in a lousy desert. There's no water. We're going to die out here. Why didn't you just leave us in Egypt, Moses? At least we had water there!" All of a sudden Moses was surrounded by angry people, fists shaking in the air, "Wa-ter, Wa-ter!" they chanted.

"God, HELP ME! These people are getting angrier by the minute," Moses quickly prayed. "What am I going to do? There isn't any water around here. But, if you don't do something, they're going to stone me to death!" God answered right away, "Take some of the leaders and go to Mt. Sinai. I'll meet you by a big rock there."

Quickly Moses called the leaders together and they left the shouting mob behind. "Moses, this is the rock," God said. "Hit it with your shepherd's staff." Moses could hear the angry people behind him as he lifted his staff and slammed it down on the rock. Just as it cracked against the stone, water gushed from the rock. Everyone drank all they wanted. Once again, God had taken care of his people . . . and helped Moses.

Based on Exodus 17:1-6

Becoming a Man of God
A man of God sees God's power.

How many times were the Israelites going to complain about the way things were going for them? When Moses first told them that God had called him to lead them out of Egypt, he did a miracle to prove God was with him. Then, God sent ten terrible plagues on the Egyptians to convince Pharaoh to let the people go. Next, God parted the waters of the Red Sea to save them from the Egyptian army. But, the Israelites must have had very short memories, because at the slightest little problem, they started complaining and shouting at Moses again. That must have made God very sad.

But, every time the Israelites complained, Moses turned to God and asked, "What do I do now?" Each time, God answered Moses' problem with a wonderful miracle. Imagine the people's surprise when Moses smacked the rock with his shepherd's staff and water poured out. God is really awesome, isn't he?

Think about examples of God's power that you have seen. If you haven't seen a "miracle" then think about the everyday displays of his power, in weather or in the sun coming up every day. What are some other God-power-shows?

Dad's Turn

Have you ever been on a camping trip where you were hot and tired and thirsty? Tell your son about the experience. Did you ever get frustrated with the leaders because of your discomfort?

When have you been most impressed with God's power? Have you been obviously aware of God's power in your life? Tell your son about it, share with him how God's power is evident and important in your life. Talk with your son about God's power. Talk about how God's power so often takes care of us. Some things we take for granted that keep us safe every day—warmth from the sun, gravity to keep us in place, air to breathe. Talk about awesome displays of God's power, such as lightning storms, volcanoes, tornadoes, and gentle displays of his power, such as beautiful sunsets or the creation of something as delicate as a butterfly.

A Verse to Remember
Power, O God, belongs to you.
Psalm 62:11

Yellow-bellied chickens!

"You've dragged us all over this wilderness in search of the Promised Land," a man complained to Moses. "We're tired of searching, we want to see it."

"Funny you should say that," Moses smiled, "because we're here. We're right outside the Promised Land. God wants you to see how great it is, so I'm sending in twelve spies to see what the land is like and how well the cities are protected. Then, we'll know what we're getting into before we attack."

A few days later the twelve spies were sneaking into the country, sliding down mountains, crossing over rivers, seeing what the land was like. "Wow! Look at the size of those grapes over there!" one spy called. "Let's take some back to show Moses and the rest of the people. This land is incredible!" Everywhere the men searched, the land looked great . . . except for the really, really big people who lived there.

"We're back!" Forty days after sneaking into the Promised Land, the spies returned to Moses and the Israelites, carrying the giant grapes on their shoulders. "The land is awesome. It's like nothing you've seen before . . . good crops, good water . . .but . . ."

"When you say 'but' that means something bad! What is it?" someone called out.

"Well, there is this one little problem of the giant people who live there and the big walls around every city," one spy mumbled.

"Never mind that," Joshua and Caleb shouted. "God said that the land is ours. All we have to do is trust him . . . and go for it!"

"Don't be crazy!" the other ten spies cried out, with their chicken hearts on their sleeves. "There's no way we could beat those giants!" The people listened as the ten spies argued with the two spies.

Finally they said, "Majority rules. There's no way we're going to try to capture the land!"

Caleb and Joshua were so frustrated that they wanted to stomp on all the giant grapes. "Why couldn't the people just trust God?"

God was even more frustrated than they were, "I told you I was giving you the land. Since you don't believe me, you can just wander around in the desert for forty years. Then, I'll give the land to your children. All of you, except Caleb and Joshua, will be dead. They are the only two who can see the Promised Land.

Based on Numbers 13-14

Becoming a Man of God
A man of God trusts God.

What was it going to take to get the Israelites to actually trust God? He already told them that he was giving them the land of Canaan, but only Moses, Joshua and Caleb believed him. The rest of the spies and all the people were yellow-bellied chickens!

Of course, trust isn't easy because it means believing someone will (or can) do what they say they will do . . . even when you can't actually see anything happening. Trust is hard the first time you trust someone, but, the Israelites had certainly seen God's power before this. They should have been able to trust him to give them the land of Canaan.

Have you ever trusted someone to do something, then been disappointed because they didn't come through? How did you feel? Have you ever trusted someone to keep a promise and they did? How did you feel then?

Dad's Turn

Are you a trusting person? Do you trust people to keep their word or follow through on what they tell you? Tell your son about a time when someone made a promise to you and did follow through on it? How did you feel? Remind him of a promise you once made to him that you kept. Ask him if that made him more willing to trust you the next time?

Remind your son of the many promises God gives us in his word-his promise to forgive our sins, to love us, to help us with our problems. Share with him that the stories in the Bible are examples of the way God keeps his word . . . so we know we can trust him! Trusting God gives great peace and comfort that he will answer prayers and keep the promises he has already given in his word.

A Verse to Remember

The LORD your God is indeed God. He is the faithful God who keeps his covenant for a thousand generations and constantly loves those who love him and obey his commands.

Deuteronomy 7:9

Whiners and Complainers

"Where are you taking us now? Are we ever going to stop walking around this desert?" Everywhere Moses turned someone was whining and complaining. "Why did you bring us out of Egypt anyway?" "Yeah," someone else jumped in, "it wasn't so bad being slaves . . . at least we had food and water!"

"Yeah . . . real food! I'm sick of this manna stuff."

"Aarrghh," Moses was so frustrated, "you wouldn't even have manna if it wasn't for God. He sends you that food from heaven every day."

"But day in and day out it's manna, manna, manna. I remember fresh fruit and meat. We used to have something different every day!" another man shouted.

God heard the people complaining about the very miracles he was doing to take care of them. He knew that he had to do something to get their attention again. The people walked down into a small valley, still complaining and whining, and suddenly there were snakes everywhere, even in the trees and high up on the rocks. They couldn't get away from the snakes.

"Aaaahhh, that snake bit me! Help me, I'm going to die!"
People everywhere were screaming and crying for help.
"Moses, pray that God will take the snakes away. Please,
we're sorry for complaining so much. Ask him to help us!"
Just as he had so many times already, Moses asked God to
help the people.

"Make a fake snake that looks just like these snakes and put it on a tall pole. The people simply have to look at it and their snakebites will be healed," God said. Moses made a snake out of bronze and told the people to look at it.

"Just looking at a bronze snake will heal us?" the people were amazed. But, everyone who obeyed the command was healed. Once again God saved his people.

Based on Numbers 21:4-9

Becoming a Man of God
A man of God doesn't complain.

Those Israelites complained about everything, didn't they? Every time Moses turned around they had some new complaint. God was sending them food from heaven every single day, and they complained that they had to eat the same thing every day.

Moses, on the other hand, was better at looking at the blessings God was giving them every day and being thankful for God's love and care. Like the old saying, Moses looked at the glass of water and saw it as half full, but the Israelites saw it as half empty.

Do you complain about stuff? Come on, be honest. A good clue would be if you've heard your parents tell you to stop whining. What kinds of things do you complain about? Is it usually because you want your way about something, or because someone doesn't do what you want exactly when you want them to?

Dad's Turn

All of us are guilty of complaining at some time. Tell your son about a time when you complained. Why were you unhappy with the situation? Were you later sorry for complaining? How did the people around you handle your attitude?

Point out that, even though the Israelites were complaining again, God once again met their need. He did another miracle to save them—but they had a part in this miracle. They had to actually look at the bronze snake in order to be healed from a snakebite. So, while God did do a miracle, the people had to believe that he was offering a way to save them. Again and again God sent the message, "Trust me!"

Does your son have a habit of complaining? Talk to him about it now. Help him begin to see that complaining is a selfish habit. Talk to him about learning to be patient and wait for his requests to be answered. Talk about trusting God to answer his prayers. Sometimes it takes lots of patience and trust to wait on God for his timing in answering our prayers—and we shouldn't be complaining in the meantime.

A Verse to Remember

The LORD is wonderfully good to those who wait for him and seek him.

Lamentations 3:25

The Donkey and the Angel

"King Balak wants to see me. ME!" Balaam was pretty excited. But God said, "Don't go to Balak. He wants you to hurt my people."

Even so, early the next morning Balaam climbed on his donkey and headed out to see the king. God was not happy with him.

God doesn't want him to go...

Balaam hummed a tune as he rode along. "Balak promised me lots of money for my help and I can think of lots of ways to spend it," he thought. But, suddenly Balaam's donkey bolted off the road and into a field. "What are you doing?" Balaam shouted, hitting the donkey with a stick and pulling it back to the road.

"What was that all about?" Balaam wondered. "OWWW," he screamed as the donkey slammed his leg into a wall. "There's plenty of room between these buildings. Why are you smashing me into the wall?" Balaam beat the donkey again.

A few minutes later the donkey laid down in the middle of the road and nothing Balaam did would make him get up. Balaam raised his arm to beat the donkey again, but his arm stopped in midair when the donkey said, "Why are you hitting me? I'm just trying to protect you."

"Did you just . . . speak?" Balaam was pretty confused—
whoever heard of a talking donkey? Just then God let Balaam
see what the donkey had been seeing all along . . . an angel
in the middle of the road holding a sword high in the air. "Oh
wow! I was disobeying God by going to see the king. You
saved me from God's anger!" Balaam realized. Now Balaam
was thankful for his donkey's stubbornness.

Based on Numbers 22:21-34

Becoming a Man of God
A man of God keeps his priorities straight.

Balaam got his priorities messed up. Do you wonder what that means? Balaam knew in his heart that the most important thing was to obey God. But, when King Balak offered him lots of money to do what he wanted, Balaam forgot about obeying God. He got dollar signs in his eyes!

God got his attention in a pretty cool way, didn't he? A talking donkey! Wow! God gave Balaam a second chance to obey him, by letting the donkey see the angel in the road and doing what it could to stop Balaam from going to the king.

What do you think should be the most important thing for you to do? Obey God? Obey your parents? Is it ever hard for you to do that because your friends or brothers or sisters try to get you to disobey? Or is it ever hard because something you want to do looks so appealing . . . even though it would be disobeying to do it?

Dad's Turn

It may not be easy for you to admit to your son that you sometimes get your priorities mixed up. But, more than likely you have at one time or another. Tell your son about it. Perhaps you once got so caught up in your career that your relationship with your family was sacrificed. Maybe it became more important to make money than to spend time with God. Tell your son how you came to realize your priorities were wrong. What did you do once you made that realization?

Make a list together of things that are important to you and your son. Now, prioritize that list. Talk about how to keep things in perspective and keep the thing in first place that should be there.

A Verse to Remember
Seek his will in all you do, and he will direct your paths.
Proverbs 3:6

Million Man March

God never forgets. He promised to give the Israelites their own land and even though it had been a long time, he hadn't forgotten that promise. Joshua was the Israelites' leader, since Moses died. "God wants us to set up camp outside the city of Jericho," he announced to his people.

"That city is locked up tight and has big walls around it," one man said.

"That's OK. God says that Jericho will be ours. We must trust him and do exactly what he tells us to do," Joshua answered.

"All right!" the people shouted, high-fiving each other and celebrating. "Those Jericho-ites won't even know what hit them!" "Yeah, we're going to do some serious city-capturing!"

"Hold on," Joshua stopped the celebration. "We're going to do exactly what God says. He wants us to march around the city once a day for six days—and not say a word!"

"What? The men of Jericho will think we're crazy!" "Yeah, we'll look like fools!" the people complained. But, Joshua wouldn't budge, "It's God's way or no way!"

"HA! Look at those crazy Israelites!" the men of Jericho laughed. "What are they trying to do, shake the walls and make them fall down?"

Once a day for six days the Israelites silently marched around the city, then went back to their camp. By the sixth day, the men of Jericho were making so much fun of them that the Israelites wondered if Joshua really knew what he was doing.

The seventh day the people of Jericho woke up to the sound of the Israelites marching again. "Why don't they go away?" people moaned, as they rolled over and went back to sleep. Some people did notice that the Israelites didn't stop after one time around. "Ahh, it's just some new wrinkle in their silly plan," they thought. Six times Joshua led the people around the city. By then, crowds of people were on the walls making fun of the army and throwing water and other stuff at them. But, even with water dripping in his eyes, Joshua kept marching.

"Hey, fools, you're gonna wear out your shoes with all that marching!" the men of Jericho called.

When the Israelites started their seventh time around the city, Joshua called, "Shout, the Lord has given you this city!" The Israelites gave out a loud, "Whoop!" and the priests blared on their horns. The men standing on the big walls fell off as the walls crumbled and fell. The Israelites raced in and captured Jericho. God gave them the city, just as he said.

Based on Joshua 6

Becoming a Man of God
A man of God does exactly what God says.

The Israelites seem to be learning to trust . . . trust their leader and trust God. When they heard that God was giving them the city of Jericho, they were ready to take it by storm. They even wanted to gloat a little bit . . . kind of rub it in to the men of Jericho that they were going to capture that city, no matter what! They wanted to have a real show of power. But, God had other ideas. He wanted the people to know that Jericho was being captured by his power—not theirs.

So, when Joshua laid down the law—it's God's way or no way, the Israelites agreed. Don't you imagine that they felt silly marching around the city walls every day for six days, but not saying a word, not shooting an arrow, not doing anything but marching? But, God was true to his word. The city was theirs, and there was no doubt that it was because of God's power!

How good are you at following instructions? Do you find it hard to exactly follow what you are told to do? When was a time that you didn't follow instructions, and later were sorry? When was a time that you did follow instructions exactly, and were glad?

Dad's Turn

Dad, do you read the instructions before you assemble a piece of furniture, or before using a new appliance? Is reading the instructions a last resort for you? Tell your son about a time when your neglect to follow instructions caused a problem. What happened? Did it cause you extra work to correct the situation? Were you sorry that you didn't follow instructions?

Remind your son of a time when he followed instructions you gave him. Tell him how pleased you were with his attention to detail and obedience. Tell him how proud you were of him.

God is pleased with us when we follow instructions he gives us. His instructions are given in the Bible. One good place to look at his instructions are the Ten Commandments—good instructions for how to live for him and how to treat other people. It's important to exactly follow his instructions, and not try to reword them to fit the way we live.

A Verse to Remember

Teach me to do your will, for you are my God.
Psalm 143:10

The Longest Day

Spears soared through the air and swords clashed! Joshua's army won another battle. His army of Israelites destroyed or captured every enemy they fought against. The king of Gibeon heard about Joshua's victories . . . and offered to be friends. "It's better to fight with them than against them!" he told his soldiers.

"Hey, if we're going to stand any chance against Joshua's army, we've got to forget our differences and fight together as one army," Adoni-zedek, the king of Jerusalem explained his plan to four other Amorite kings. "Let's attack Gibeon and capture their army. That will bring Joshua's army down to a normal size."

When the Amorites attacked, the king of Gibeon sent a
message to Joshua asking for help. "Come on, men. We've got
to help our friends!" Joshua and the Israelites traveled all
night to Gibeon. Their early morning attack surprised the
Amorites and the battle began!

"Let's get out of here. We can't beat these guys!" The Amorites took off running, but as they ran . . . "OW, now it's hailing huge hailstones. What else can go wrong?" The Amorites knew they were never going to beat Joshua's army. God sent the biggest, hardest hailstones ever. More soldiers were killed by hailstones than in the battle.

"Wow, it feels like we've been fighting for hours. But, the sun hasn't even moved, so it can't have been that long," one Israelite soldier said, dropping to the ground for a rest.

"No, it has been a long time. Before the battle, Joshua asked God to make the sun and moon stand still until we won—and God did!

(Never before that time, and never since has God made the sun and moon stand still!)

Based on Joshua 10:1-15

Becoming a Man of God
A man of God isn't afraid to ask for a miracle.

Joshua really wanted to win this battle. He knew that his army was the army of God and he didn't want God's enemies to defeat him. He also knew that if the battle wasn't won by sundown, it would stop for the day because they couldn't fight in the dark. It might pick up the next day, or it might just be considered a tie and never be continued. Joshua really wanted to WIN!

So, he asked God to do a miracle. He asked him to keep daylight shining until the battle was won . . . and God did! Joshua believed that God has that kind of power and that he is willing to share that power with his people, if we ask him to.

Have you ever asked God to do a miracle? Did you believe in your heart that he could do it, and that he would? What was your request? What happened?

Dad's Turn

If you have a true story of a miracle God did in response to
your prayer, tell your son about it. When was a time when
you sincerely prayed for God to do a miracle? What
happened? We often pray for God to supernaturally heal a
loved one, or show his power in some supernatural way, as
he did for Joshua. In our world today, miracles are often
explained away or denied. Help your son understand, that the
God of the Old Testament can still do miracles in our world,
if he chooses to do so. But, remind your son that if God
doesn't answer his prayers with a miracle, it doesn't mean he
isn't listening. It only means that the miracle wasn't in his
plans.

Look at some situations you have prayed for, and see
if you can pick out small answers to prayer, even if God
didn't send the "big miracle" you asked for.

A Verse to Remember

We can be confident that he will listen to us whenever we
ask him for anything in line with his will.

1 John 5:14

Battle Plan!

"Send out the word! Every able bodied man must join the army! We're going to beat those Midianites once and for all!" Gideon was determined to have the biggest army Israel had ever seen! Soon more than 30,000 men were ready to fight.

"Uh uh," God said. "If you win with that many soldiers, the Israelites will think they won without my help. Some of the soldiers have to go."

"OK," Gideon agreed. "Anyone who is scared can go home," he shouted. Twenty thousand men left.

"Take your 10,000 men down to the river and tell them to get a drink," God said. While the men drank, Gideon walked around watching them.

"What's he looking at?" one soldier whispered. "I don't know, but I feel weird with him watching every move I make," another answered.

Suddenly Gideon shouted, "Every man who scooped water up in his hands must stay. Everyone else can go home." Now Gideon's army was down to 300 soldiers.

"We're going to whip those Midianites!" Gideon promised. "I know there are thousands more of them than there are of us. But, God is fighting on our side! Count off by threes, and go stand with your group. This is how we're going to win . . ." Gideon told the soldiers the plan that God had given him.

Around midnight the soldiers sneaked up on the Midianites. Each one carried a horn and a torch covered with a clay jar. One soldier bumped his jar against something and the "ping" rang out in the darkness. "Shh! We gotta be quiet until Gideon gives us the sign." Just then Gideon shouted and according to the battle plan, they broke the jars. The glowing torches and tooting horns scared the Midianites. They ran all over each other in their hurry to get away. Gideon's little army won!

Based on Judges 7

Becoming a Man of God
A man of God trusts God's power.

Gideon had a good plan . . . get the biggest army together he could, then attack the enemy and beat them soundly!

But, God had a different plan. He wanted everyone to know that this battle would be won by his power, not because Gideon had a big army. Imagine how the soldiers who remained felt as Gideon kept sending other soldiers home. They saw their army dwindle down to 300 men from 30,000. Do you think they were scared? Do you think they felt like they didn't have a chance against the big Midianite army? When God decides to do something, it will happen, however he chooses.

The whole foundation of life with God is that you must trust him. Trust his word, his power, and his love. Think about a time when you've seen God's power displayed. How did it make you feel?

Dad's Turn

"Trust God" . . . easy words to say, aren't they? But, sometimes they aren't so easy to live out. Can you recall a time from your childhood when you needed and found God's power? How about when your family moved to a new town and you really needed some new friends? Did you pray about it? Then, all of a sudden a week or so later, did you realize that God had given you new friends? Was that coincidence, or a display of God's power in the hearts of your new friends?

In our world, we tend to think that bigger is better. Can you and your son think of some examples of times when bigger is not better? Why is it important to know that things happen because of God's power and not because of ours? When you know that God's power is working, does that make it easier to trust him the next time?

A Verse to Remember

So be strong and take courage, all you who put your hope in the LORD.

Psalm 31:24

The Strongest Man in the World

"BOING! Boing, Boing!" The full-grown lion bounced across the ground like a toy. The surprised look on it's face showed that it had no idea it had attacked Samson—the strongest man in the world! No one, not even a full-grown lion could match Samson's strength. He was a giant of a man with muscles that rippled and bulged. But, Samson did have a weakness . . . pretty girls. He liked to tease them and he liked it when they teased him back. This was something that would get him in big, big trouble!

One day Samson fell head-over-heels in love with a beautiful lady. Delilah was a Philistine—a group of people who didn't believe in God, didn't trust God, didn't live for God—and Samson had no business spending time with her. (He should have known better.) There was one other problem . . . the Philistines HATED Samson. He had once killed a whole bunch of Philistines with a donkey's jawbone, and their relatives were looking for some way to get even with him.

The sneaky Philistines came up with a plan. They paid Delilah lots of money to find out the secret of Samson's strength. Then they were going to trick him and capture him. Delilah snuggled up to Samson, with dollar signs shining in her eyes, "What makes you so strong, big guy?" she whispered.

Samson thought she was being funny, so every time she asked, he gave her some silly answer like, "Tie me up with seven bowstrings and I'll be as weak as a baby, or new ropes will hold me down!" 'Course every time Delilah tried what he said, he escaped like he had been held with tiny threads.

Finally, Delilah started to cry, "If you loved me, you would tell me the truth."

Samson couldn't take the tears, so he confessed, "The secret of my strength is my long hair. It's never been cut and that shows that I'm devoted to God."

Later, while Samson took a nap, Delilah took out a huge knife and chopped his hair off. "Come on boys, and bring your money," she called to the Philistines. Samson was captured.

The Philistines threw Samson in jail and only brought him out when they wanted to make fun of him. At one party, they laughed at him, then stood him over in a corner. "God, help me one last time to beat the Philistines," Samson prayed. He was sorry that his weakness for pretty women had made him sin. He put one hand on each of the big columns that held up the ceiling and pushed with all his strength. God gave him one last bit of strength and the columns broke! The ceiling crashed down into the room, killing all the Philistines. . . and Samson. But, as he died he killed more Philistines than he had in his whole life.

Based on Judges 16

Becoming a Man of God
A man of God gets a second chance.

The great thing about this story is that when Samson messed up by getting involved with a Philistine woman, God didn't give up on him. He got a second chance to make things right and to do God's work.

That's pretty encouraging, isn't it? We all mess up sometimes and make bad choices. But, God doesn't throw up his hands in disgust and walk away. He never gives up on us, we get a second chance, a third chance . . . however many chances we need to do God's work or to learn more about living for him.

Samson had a weakness for pretty girls. What's your weakness? What tempts you to do wrong or to forget about God for a while? Is there one friend who seems to always get you in trouble? Or is there a video game or TV show that you easily get wrapped up in so you forget to do homework or chores that Mom and Dad give you?

Dad's Turn

Tell your son about a time when you messed up big time, but were given a second chance to do better. Remind him of a time when he messed up by not obeying. Did you stop loving him because he messed up? Did you give him a second chance?

Help him understand that we all make mistakes, bad choices, or just get lazy about doing what we know is right. But, God doesn't give up on us and the people who love us don't give up on us either.

Ask your son if there is anything in his life that is a weakness for him. . . a temptation that keeps him from doing his jobs or from doing what is right. Help him come up with a plan to be strong against this temptation. Pray about it together.

A Verse to Remember
Be very careful to love the LORD your God.
Joshua 23:11

A Voice in the Darkness

Samuel always said his prayers before bedtime, "God bless Momma and keep her safe. God bless Mr. Eli and take care of him . . . and God bless me and help me learn everything I can to be your servant. Amen." Little Samuel lived in the temple with the priest, Eli, because his momma had promised God that if he gave her a son, she would give him back to serve God. So, Samuel learned everything Eli taught him. He was a good boy and he took his work very seriously.

After one especially long day of temple work, Samuel was snoozing away, when something interrupted his sleep. He rolled over and rubbed his eyes awake. "Samuel, Samuel." Someone was calling his name. Climbing out of bed and sliding into his slippers he ran to Eli's room, "Yes, Sir, what do you want?"

The funny thing was, Eli was still snoring away. He hadn't called Samuel! "Go back to bed," Eli mumbled.

"That was weird," Samuel thought as he climbed under the blankets once again. He was just dozing off when he heard, "Samuel, Samuel." Jumping out of bed, he dashed to Eli's room, knocking his knee on the door frame. "Owww," he moaned. "Eli, what do you want?" he asked with a little impatience creeping into his voice.

"Why do you keep waking me up? I didn't call you. Go back to bed!" Eli sounded a little impatient, too.

"That was weirder than ever," Samuel thought. "Am I dreaming this or what?" He sat on the edge of his bed for awhile trying to figure out what was going on. Finally, he got so sleepy that he fell over on the pillow. A gentle voice woke him up, "Samuel, Samuel."

"This isn't funny!" he announced loudly, stomping into Eli's room. "Yes?" he asked, a bit loudly. Now the old priest knew what was going on. He told Samuel exactly what to do when he heard the voice again.

Samuel got back into bed, but he didn't go to sleep. He lay very still, waiting for the voice to speak again. Sure enough, he heard, "Samuel, Samuel."

"Yes, Lord, I'm listening," he answered, just as Eli had told him to do. "Eli was right, the voice is from God. I wonder what God wants to say to me," Samuel wondered. He listened very carefully to everything God said. That night Samuel learned an important lesson about listening when God calls.

Based on 1 Samuel 3

Becoming a Man of God
A man of God listens for God's voice.

Samuel was just a little boy who heard God call his name. That might be something you would expect to happen to an adult, but not a child. What would God want with a child? Why would he choose to speak to a child instead of an adult. Well, God looks at a person's heart to see if they truly love and care about him. He saw that Samuel did, so he trusted Samuel with an important message.

It is important to know that Samuel would not have heard God's message if he hadn't been quiet so he could hear God's voice. Also, when Eli told him what to do to hear God's message, Samuel did it.

Have you ever dreamed something that seemed so real that you were sure it had actually happened? Maybe that's how Samuel felt. Samuel found out that it was God's voice speaking to him because he was quiet and listened for him.

Dad's Turn

How good are you at listening? When your son talks to you, do you listen with full attention? Do you really hear what he says or do you partially listen to him while you are doing something else at the same time?

Tell your son about a time when you only partially listened to instructions or news, and later were sorry that you didn't have all the information.

Talk to your son about spending time in silence, where you can hear God speak to you. Together read a verse of Scripture, then just be quiet together while you each think about what it means.

A Verse to Remember
Be silent and know that I am God.
Psalm 46:10

Bigger Isn't Always Better!

"Are you big, strong soldiers really afraid of that guy?" David asked King Saul's soldiers. "I heard that creep has been making fun of God and this army two times a day for the last forty days. Why doesn't someone stop him?" No one answered young David. Every single soldier suddenly got very busy studying some little speck of dust on the ground. They knew David was right. They were all scared of big, ugly, creepy Goliath.

"Well, I'm not scared of that creep . . . and I'm just a kid!" David announced to anyone who might be listening. Suddenly a hand grabbed his shoulder and squeezed it . . . HARD. "Why don't you just go home, you little bragger?" It was David's older brother and he was MAD! "Just go home. You don't have any business being here."

"Oh, I'll go alright . . . but not home," David shouted. "I'm gonna fight that giant!"

King Saul was excited when he heard that someone had volunteered to fight Goliath. "Send the brave soldier to me!" he ordered. He almost dropped his royal teeth when David walked in.

"You're just a kid. You can't fight a 9-foot-tall giant!" However, he had to admit there was steely determination in David's eyes when he said, "Yes, I can!"

"Hmm, what are my options?" the king thought. He had to admit there weren't many. "OK, but at least wear my armor," he said. David put it on, but it was so big and heavy that he couldn't even move. "Get me outta this!" he shouted. "I've gotta do this my way!"

David climbed out of King Saul's armor and headed down the hill toward Goliath. On the way, he picked up some rocks. Dropping one into his slingshot, he fixed his eyes on Goliath and marched on.

When Goliath saw the kid with the slingshot coming toward him, he got MAD! "Come on, kid. I'm gonna tear you to shreds!" the big creep shouted. He pounded his chest and flexed his giant muscles. David kept right on walking . . . King Saul's soldiers hid their eyes.

David began to swing his slingshot around and around over his head. It seemed like Goliath couldn't take his eyes off it. They flew back and forth in their sockets, watching the sling's every move. When David let go, the rock flew from the sling and soared through the air. It landed with a sickening THUD right on Goliath's forehead. The 9-foot-tall giant looked completely shocked as he fell to the ground.

King Saul's soldiers jumped to life, shouting, "He won! The little guy won!" David smiled because he knew the truth—he didn't win—God did.

Based on 1 Samuel 18

Becoming a Man of God
A man of God knows bigger isn't always better.

Imagine how Goliath felt when he saw a skinny little kid walking toward him after King Saul's entire army had been afraid to fight him. He was probably insulted because he felt his power deserved King Saul's best soldier, not some kid. Maybe he felt like the Israelites were making fun of him. One thing is for sure, he was absolutely positive that he would beat David! Ha! He didn't know who he was dealing with, did he?

David wasn't an idiot, he knew that Goliath was bigger and stronger. He knew that Goliath was an experienced soldier. But, he also knew that he had God on his side—and that is all he needed!

You can't always judge a situation or a person by how things look on the outside. If that were true, Goliath would have beaten David, hands down! But, the youngest, smallest, weakest person who has God on his side can do whatever God wants him to do!

Have you ever had to do something really hard that frightened you? Did you ask for God's help? How did he help you?

Dad's Turn

It's easy for a little guy to believe that bigger is better. Talk about how boys change as they grow into men. How strong is a little boy compared to a grown-up man? Arm wrestle with your son and let him see how easily you can defeat him. Tell him that he will get stronger as he gets older, too. Give him an example of how God's power helped you do something that you wouldn't have been able to do alone.

Ask your son what kinds of situations he finds difficult as a young boy. Talk through what it is that makes the situation difficult. Pray together for God's help and strength and for your son to know for sure that God is helping him.

A Verse to Remember

When I am afraid, I put my trust in you.
Psalm 56:3

Wisdom and Love

King Solomon was very smart and very rich. People all over the world had heard about his incredible wisdom and his beautiful palace. He made good choices and good decisions. His wisdom and riches were gifts from God. The good king used his wisdom to help people whenever he could. One day a very sad mother came to King Solomon with a terrible problem.

"O great King, please help me," the woman said. She pointed to another woman who was holding a small baby. "That woman stole my baby," she whispered.

"Did not!" the woman said, hugging the baby tightly.

"We both had babies," the first woman continued. "During the night her baby died. So, she took my live baby and put her dead child beside me."

"NO!" screamed the second woman. "She's lying! She's trying to steal my baby!"

The great and wise king looked at both women and thought for a few moments about how to handle the situation. Both women jumped when he loudly commanded, "Bring a sword. Cut this child in two and give half to each woman!" For a few seconds it seemed that no one in the room even breathed.

"NO!" the first woman screamed. "Don't hurt him, please don't hurt the baby! Let her keep him." She fell to the floor, sobbing and crying.

Everyone was amazed, when, at the very same time the second woman held the baby out to the guard. "Fine!" she shouted. "Kill him. If I can't have him, then neither can she!"

King Solomon smiled calmly. "Stop," he commanded. "Give the child to the first woman. She is the true mother."

She looked up at the king in amazement. "How do you know that for sure?" she whispered through her tears.

King Solomon took her hand and pulled her to her feet. "Because the real mother would rather give up her child than let him be hurt," he said. The woman hugged her child, knowing deep in her heart that the king's great wisdom was truly a gift from God.

Based on 1 Kings 3:16-28

Becoming a Man of God
A man of God helps others.

King Solomon's wisdom was a gift from God. He treasured this gift and used it to help other people, not just for his own benefit. He knew that the child's real mother would do pretty much anything to save her child and keep him safe. He also knew that the other woman wouldn't care if the child was killed.

God gives each of his children different gifts and talents. It must make him happy when we use those gifts and talents to help others. The more we help one another the better life is for all of us.

How do you help other people? What are some things you could do for your family or neighbors, even as a child? How do others help you? What do your family members do for you?

Dad's Turn

If your son sees you helping people whenever you can, he will learn to do the same thing. Tell him about a time that you feel good about when you went out of your way to help someone. How did the other person feel? How did you feel? Tell him about a time when someone helped you. How did you feel? What are the skills or talents you have that you willingly share with others?

Talk with your son about ways he can help other people. What are some practical things he can do for the family or for elderly neighbors? How can you and your son increase your level of wisdom? Talk about topics you both would like to know more about. Can you read books or watch videos about these topics? Decide on a plan for increasing your knowledge of God and his word. Are there other books besides this one that can help you know God better?

A Verse to Remember

Two people can accomplish more than twice as much as one; they get a better return for their labor. If one person falls, the other can reach out and help. But people who are alone when they fall are in real trouble.

Ecclesiastes 4:9-10

Raining Fire

"If God is truly God then worship him and forget your fake gods!" Elijah shouted. "You claim to serve God one day, but the next day you're worshipping an idol. Make up your minds!" Elijah was the only prophet of God left. But there were 450 prophets of the fake god, Baal, who were always teaching about how powerful and wonderful Baal was. "It's time for a showdown," Elijah decided. "I challenge you Baal prophets to a contest. Meet me on Mt. Carmel and we'll see whose god is the real God!"

The prophets of Baal were sure they would win this contest, after all it was 450 to one! So, they did exactly what Elijah told them to do—built an altar and put a bull on it. Then they danced around and shouted to Baal, "Send fire down and burn up our offering. Come on Baal . . . yoohoo . . . oh, B-a-a-l!" Elijah sat near a tree and watched them.

Finally, he said, "Maybe we should have checked with Baal first. Maybe he's gone on vacation. Maybe he's sleeping . . . or in the bathroom."

Elijah let them try all day before saying, "Enough already.
Baal isn't going to answer. It's my turn."

    Then he built an altar, just like theirs. He put a bull on
it, just like theirs. But, he also dug a trench around his altar
and poured four big jars of water over the whole thing. Then,
four more jars . . . and four more. The wood, the bull and the
ground were nearly floating in water.

Elijah stepped back and said, "OK God, show these people that you are the true and powerful God." Instantly flames of fire rained down from heaven and burned up the bull, the altar and even the water!

"W-w-wh-a-a-at was that?" the prophets of Baal asked each other. One of them crept up and touched the stone altar. "OW! That thing is HOT!"

All 450 prophets stared at the smoky altar for a long time. They couldn't believe what they had seen with their own eyes. Suddenly one of them shouted, "Let's get outta here!" and all 450 took off down the mountain.

Meanwhile, the people who had come to watch the contest dropped to their knees in awe. "The Lord is God. The Lord is God," they shouted.

Based on 1 Kings 18:19-40

Becoming a Man of God
A man of God stands up for God.

Pretty scary odds, huh? One prophet of God against 450 prophets of Baal. But, Elijah was sick and tired of the people ignoring God and paying attention to the fake gods. He knew it was time to take a stand and let God show his power. He also knew that Baal was no match for the true God. Elijah took a stand, because he wanted the people to see once and for all who the true God was. Now, the prophets of Baal could have gotten mad at Elijah and tried to hurt him, but he wasn't afraid. He knew that God would take care of him.

Have you ever taken a stand for something, even if your friends thought it was dumb? Do any of your friends make fun of you for going to church or caring about God? It's not easy to stand up against other people, is it?

Dad's Turn

Has there ever been a time when you saw people making fun of someone or something and it upset you? Did you get involved to stop the situation and take a stand? How did it go? Were you nervous about your safety? How did you feel when it was all over?

If your son has taken a stand for something with his friends, praise him for that. Encourage him to continue doing so. Talk about ways your son can take a stand for God. Could he invite a friend to Sunday school or Vacation Bible school? Could he share a children's Bible or storybook with a friend? Encourage him to be kind and respectful when he chooses to take a stand on any subject.

A Verse to Remember

I can do everything with the help of Christ who gives me the strength I need.

Philippians 4:13

One "Hot" Rod!

"Elijah, teach me everything you know about serving God,"
Elisha begged. "I'm not going to let you out of my sight. I
want to learn everything you know. If God sends you away
someplace, I'm coming with you!"

It almost seemed like Elisha knew that his great
teacher, Elijah, wasn't going to be around much longer. He
wanted to learn as much as he could from the great prophet
of God.

For the next few weeks Elisha followed Elijah everywhere. It never failed though, when they went to a new town, someone would say to him, "Did you know that God is going to take your master away very soon?"

"Of course I know that," Elisha always answered. He hardly even slept at night because he was afraid he would miss learning something about Elijah's close walk with God.

One afternoon Elijah and Elisha were walking near the Jordan River when Elijah stopped, took off his robe, and carefully folded it. "What is he doing?" Elisha wondered. When Elijah slapped the robe on the water, water splashed in Elisha's face. He wiped the water from his face and looked back at the river. "Wow! The waters divided and where there used to be water, the ground is now dry!" Elijah smiled and stepped between the waters. Elisha followed him through the Jordan River.

After they crossed the river Elijah asked, "What do you want me to do for you before I leave?"

"I want to be God's prophet like you are," Elisha answered.

"That's a big request. But, if you actually see me leave, then God will give you that request." Just then, a fiery chariot swooped down between them. "What's happening?" Elisha wondered. He was terrified and his heart beat so hard that he thought it might jump out of his body! Then he realized, "Elijah is leaving in that fiery chariot!"

After the chariot disappeared, Elisha couldn't even speak, he stood staring at the sky where Elijah had disappeared. Then, he picked up Elijah's robe, folded it, and hit the water of the Jordan River. The waters parted, just as they had for Elijah. Elisha walked through the river and past a group of prophets who had seen everything that happened. He heard whispers of "Elisha has been chosen to take Elijah's place," as he passed them.

Based on 2 Kings 2

Becoming a Man of God
A man of God learns well.

Elisha seemed to know that he didn't have much time to learn from Elijah. So, he made the most of that time by staying with Elijah every moment and studying everything that the great prophet of God did. Elisha realized that he could learn a lot from the older, wiser Christian. He learned well too, which we saw when he was able to smack the robe on the waters and part the Jordan River.

Is there one person in particular who you would like to follow around and learn from the way that Elisha learned from Elijah? What kinds of things would you like to learn from that person?

Dad's Turn

Tell your son about some older person you admired as a child? What did you like about that person? What did you learn from him or her? Tell your son about the person who led you to the Lord or a special person who mentored you in your faith.

It's becoming a lost value in our society to respect older people for the wisdom we can gain by knowing them. Reinforce to your son, the respect that is due to older people. If his grandparents are still living, talk about their special gifts, talents and personalities that make them special to both of you.

Help your son think of older people who could teach him special things he would like to know such as tying flies, or carpentry. Now, who is an older Christian who could teach him things about the Christian life?

A Verse to Remember

Honor those who are your leaders in the Lord's work.
1 Thessalonians 5:12

fish food!

"No way! There is no way I'm going to Nineveh to tell those creepy people about you!" Jonah actually shouted at God. "I don't like them, and if they repented from their sins, then—I know you—you'd forgive them. So, forget it!" Jonah stomped around ranting and raving. God didn't say another word, he had told Jonah what he wanted him to do. Jonah knew what he SHOULD do . . . but that didn't mean he was going to do it!

Jonah tossed a few things in a bag and ran for the harbor. "Where you headed?" he called to the first sailor he saw.

"Tarshish," the sailor called back.

"Is that near Nineveh?" Jonah asked. When the sailor said it wasn't, Jonah hopped on board. He went down to the belly of the ship and settled in. "Hah! God can't find me here . . . and I'm NOT GOING TO NINEVEH!!!" Pretty soon the gentle rocking of the ship had lulled him to sleep.

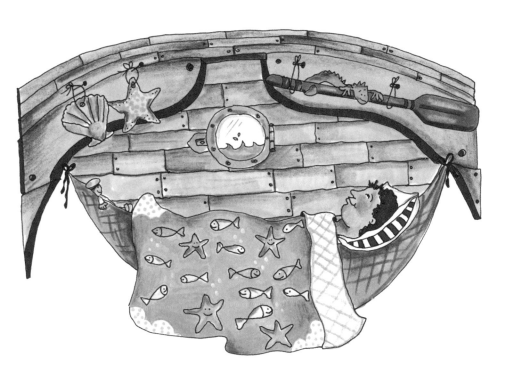

But while Jonah was sleeping, the sailors had a problem . . . a big storm just came out of nowhere and the little ship was being tossed around like a toy. "Where did this come from? The sky was clear when we set sail."

"Quit yakking about it. Toss boxes overboard. Pull down the sail. Do something or we're going to sink!" the frightened sailors worked hard to save their ship.

Jonah slept through it all . . . until a sailor shouted in his ear, "Get up! If you're a prayin' man—get to it—cause we've got trouble!"

"Oh no," Jonah thought. Right away he knew what was happening, God had found him after all. "Guys, this storm is my fault. I've been hiding from God on your ship. Just throw me overboard and the storm will stop. Everything will be OK," Jonah confessed.

None of the sailors wanted to throw Jonah into the stormy sea–they knew he would die there. But, it was pretty clear that Jonah's plan was the only way they could save their boat. So, Jonah went flying into the sea!

Jonah had barely hit the water when a gigantic fish swam up and gulped him right down. He floated in the belly of the fish for 3 days and nights, picking seaweed out of his hair and minnows from his ears. "OK, God, I know I disobeyed you and I'm sorry. If you give me another chance, I'll obey, I promise. I also promise to never eat fish again . . . yuck!" With a giant burp, the big fish spit Jonah up on the shore. True to his word, Jonah took off for Nineveh, where he taught the people about God.

Based on Jonah 1-4

Becoming a Man of God
A man of God reconsiders.

What does that word, "reconsider" mean? Jonah absolutely refused to obey God's order to go to Nineveh, and he even tried to hide from God. He ended up in the belly of a big fish with three days to think about his bad attitude and disobedience. Jonah thought about those things and he changed his mind. He "reconsidered" his decision to disobey God and decided it would be a better idea to obey. God gave him a second chance to obey. Jonah did, and the people of Nineveh heard about God's love.

When your parents ask you to do something, such as, "Pick up your toys" do you obey right away or put it off until your parents get angry at you? Do you have a problem obeying, or do you usually obey your parents or teachers right away?

Dad's Turn

There may be times when children feel that someone is always telling them what to do or giving them orders. Sometimes children may feel that they never get to make a decision on their own. That gets old and for some children, obeying is a constant challenge. Can you recall a time when you deliberately disobeyed your parents? Tell your son about it. Why didn't you want to obey? What happened when your parents discovered your disobedience? How did you feel? Did you obey your parents the next time?

If your son is very obedient, compliment him on that. If he feels that he seldom gets to make a decision, work with him to set some guidelines as to when he can make his own decisions.

Talk with him about the importance of obeying God. It's impossible to hide from God or to fool him into thinking we have obeyed when we haven't. Obeying makes everyone much happier.

A Verse to Remember

Those who obey God's word really do love him.

1 John 2:5

A Very Important Baby

Joseph always tried to do the right thing. So, when the angel told him that Mary was going to have a baby boy who was the Son of God, Joseph not only believed the angel—he went ahead with his plans to marry her. "I promise you, God, that I will be a good earthly father to your Son. I'll take good care of him!" he prayed.

Just before it was time for the baby to be born, everyone in the kingdom was ordered to go to the city where their families were from. The ruler wanted to count how many people lived in his kingdom!

"Ohhh, this baby is trying to kick his way into the world. Are we almost there?" Mary moaned.

"Yes, we'll soon be in Bethlehem and we'll get a nice room in the inn," Joseph felt bad for Mary. The baby in her tummy kicked harder with every step the donkey took. She could have stayed in Nazareth while he went for the census, but it was so close to time for the baby to be born that she didn't want to be away from him.

When they finally reached the crowded streets of Bethlehem, the town was filled with people who had come for the census. "I don't feel so good," Mary whispered, holding her hand over her mouth.

"It is pretty smelly," Joseph admitted. The scent of sweaty bodies and dirty animals even made his stomach turn a bit. "Just sit tight and I'll get us a room. Then you can rest on a soft bed." But, in only a few minutes Joseph was back with bad news, "The inn is full. There's not a room available in the whole town!"

"The innkeeper said we can stay in his stable, if we want. Mary, I'm so sorry!" Joseph felt terrible.

"It will be OK. I just want to get off this donkey," Mary moaned. In the stable Joseph pulled clean hay from the loft and made a bed for Mary, who quickly fell asleep. He was feeding the donkey when Mary cried, "The baby is coming! Oh, please, not in a stable. Joseph, do something!" But there was nothing to do, except hold her hand until the baby was born. Joseph watched in awe as Mary wrapped Jesus in strips of cloth.

"Mary, you must be exhausted," Joseph whispered. He reached to touch the baby's hand, but just then some shepherds peeked into the stable.

"An angel came to us tonight, well—hundreds of angels. They told us that this baby is the son of God, the Messiah," one shepherd said. "They said that this baby will save his people from their sins."

Joseph looked at the baby again and remembered when the angel told him that Mary's baby was the Son of God. "It's true," he thought, "this child is the Messiah."

Based on Matthew 1:20-25; Luke 2:1-20

Becoming a Man of God
A man of God recognizes his Messiah.

Joseph must have loved God and tried his best to obey him. After all, God's angel encouraged Joseph to marry young Mary and that meant he would be Jesus' earthly father. Joseph obeyed the angel and went ahead with the marriage plans. Maybe he didn't fully understand what it meant that the baby was God's Son. But, when the shepherds announced that hundreds of angels had spoken to them, Joseph must have known for sure that this baby was someone special!

Joseph took the responsibility of caring for Jesus very seriously. But, imagine how he felt when he looked at the newborn baby and understood that he was responsible for providing for and caring for the Messiah—the savior that the Jewish people had been waiting hundreds of years for.

Do you believe that Jesus is your Savior? Do you understand that the little baby whose birth we celebrate at Christmas grew up to die on a cross for your sins? Then, God brought him back to life and now he is back in heaven with God.

Dad's Turn

Tell your son a favorite childhood Christmas memory—a family tradition or a trip to grandma's house, or perhaps a program that you were part of. Tell him if your family was normally part of some holiday ministry, such as providing gifts for inner city kids. If your family isn't currently sharing in a holiday ministry, talk about something you could get involved in.

Share with your son the story of your own salvation. Tell him how you came to realize that Jesus is your Savior. How old were you? Who explained the plan of salvation to you?

Has your son made a decision for Christ? If not, talk to him about it now. Make sure he understands the plan of salvation.

A Verse to Remember

For God so loved the world that he gave his only Son, so that everyone who believes in him will not perish but have eternal life.

John 3:16

Starlight!

Amazingly, Jesus was pretty much like any other two-year-old. He liked to play with his toys. He liked to catch the soap bubbles Mary blew at him while she did laundry. The little family stayed in Bethlehem after the baby was born. Joseph set up a carpentry business and kept pretty busy, even if his kind heart sometimes made him charge less than his products were worth. Mary was happy, but sometimes she missed her mom. She wished her family could see Jesus grow up . . . and give her advice about how to be a mother.

Mary blew a bubble toward Jesus and thought about what the angel had told her and Joseph before the little guy was born. She remembered the shepherds peeking into the stable, whispering, "The Messiah. The Messiah is born. She wondered what it all meant. "I wonder what's ahead for this little guy?"

Mary and Joseph had made friends in Bethlehem. While Joseph worked away in his carpenter shop, Mary and other young mothers did their household chores. Sometimes they stopped to chat with each other and let their children play together. But, Joseph and Mary never mentioned anything to anyone about who Jesus really was.

One morning Mary heard a commotion outside. "Who are those expensive gifts for?" the neighbors whispered back and forth. Standing in the front yard were the fanciest-looking men Mary had ever seen. Soon the entire town had gathered to see what the men were going to do. "We have come from very far away to worship the child who is the king of the Jews," the strangers announced.

"Well, that should make the neighbors curious," thought Mary.

"How did you find us?" she asked. One of the men pointed to the star that was hovering right over their house. "We've been following that star for the last two years. It moved across the sky, but it stopped when it got to your house," he said. "We brought gifts for the little king."

The strangers laid gifts of gold, frankincense and myrhh in front of little Jesus. Amazingly, he seemed to understand what was happening. He didn't make a peep or move a bit. "Thank you, dear God. Thank you for this precious child," Mary's heart whispered.

Based on Matthew 2:1-12

Becoming a Man of God
A man of God gives gifts to the King.

The wise men traveled a long, long way to find young Jesus. They brought him very special gifts because they wanted to give him the best they had to give. They knew that's what he deserved. They wanted to honor the young boy who was the Savior of the world. They must have had a strong belief in and respect for God. They also honored Jesus by going home a different way instead of telling King Herod where they had found the young boy.

What gifts can you bring to Jesus? You probably don't have a job or lots of money. You can't go anywhere without your mom or dad taking you . . . so what can you give? Is he important enough to you that you want to give him gifts . . . your best gifts? List some things that you can give Jesus right now.

Dad's Turn

What is the absolute best gift you have ever received? Was it Christmas, birthday, or some other time? What made it so special? Who gave it to you? Do you still have it?

What is the best gift you've ever given to someone? Were you excited to give it? Who was it for? Why was it special?

Tell your son some of the ways you give gifts to God. Don't forget the time you give to his work at church or Sunday school. Remember everyday things like cutting an elderly neighbor's lawn, or special times when you have volunteered at a homeless shelter. Help your son see that there are many ways to give gifts to God, and not all of them involve money. He wants our hearts to love him and love other people. We can serve in that way.

Help your son complete his list of ways he can serve God. Can you think of some things you can do together?

A Verse to Remember

[God] will not forget how hard you have worked for him and how you have shown your love to him by caring for other Christians.

Hebrews 6:10

Dream Warning

Joseph loved to watch Mary play with Jesus. He enjoyed hearing the little guy's laughter and listening as Mary sang him to sleep. When the wise men came with fancy gifts for Jesus, Joseph remembered what the angel had told him about the baby being the Son of God. There was no doubt about that. Joseph took his responsibility of caring for Jesus very seriously.

A few nights after the wise men left, Joseph tumbled into bed, tired from a long day of work. He quickly fell asleep and was snoring away when a voice in his dream called, "JOSEPH!"

He groggily mumbled, "What's the matter, Mary? Is it the baby?"

"JOSEPH," the voice said again. Even in his dream, Joseph knew that wasn't Mary's voice. It was the voice of God's angel, "Take Mary and Jesus and get out of town. King Herod wants to kill the baby!" the angel said. Joseph was definitely awake now!

HURRY UP!

"Mary, wake up. Get the baby. We've got to get out of town!" Joseph called instructions as he got the donkey ready. Mary started to pack a few things before she woke the baby.

"No, we don't have time to pack. We've got to go NOW! Jesus' life is in danger!" Joseph said. That got Mary moving. In just a few minutes she was on the donkey, with the sleeping Jesus in her arms. Joseph led them into the darkness and soon Bethlehem's lights were twinkling behind them.

Joseph led his little family all the way to Egypt. They settled
in, planning to stay until the angel told them it was safe to
take Jesus back home. It was hard to live in a foreign country
where the people spoke a different language and their
customs were different. The Egyptians didn't even worship
God. Joseph and Mary trusted God for extra strength.

Finally, one night the angel came back to Joseph's
dream. "King Herod is dead," the angel said. "It's safe to take
Jesus home now."

Joseph and Mary happily packed for the trip back home. Instead of returning to Bethlehem, they went back to Nazareth where their families lived. "Momma, Poppa, I've missed you so much," Mary hugged her parents. She happily introduced them to Jesus. It was good to be home!

Based on Matthew 2:1-23

Becoming a Man of God
A man of God cares for others.

Joseph knew that he had a big responsibility. He wasn't actually Jesus' father, but he was responsible to take care of the baby, keep him safe, teach him—do all the things that a dad does. So, when the angel let Joseph know that Jesus was in danger, he did the exact right thing by immediately getting Jesus out of town. He didn't wait to see what might happen, he didn't argue with the angel, he didn't try to do things his own way by hiding Jesus somewhere in the house. He obeyed the angel's instructions to get Jesus out of town.

Who takes care of you? How do these people care for you? Do you take care of anyone or anything, such as a pet? How do you do this?

Dad's Turn

More than likely your son thinks you are pretty awesome. He probably thinks you can fix just about anything, and that you know pretty much everything. He knows that you and mom provide for the family and do everything you can to protect them and keep them safe. Tell your son about a time in your own childhood when someone took care of you. What happened? Who was your caregiver? Now, tell him about a specific time you recall when you protected or took care of him. Tell him how it made you feel to be able to take care of him.

What are some ways you and your son could take care of people outside of your family? How can you have a vision for those in your community or even in the world who have needs? How can you get involved in caring for others?

A Verse to Remember

Love each other with genuine affection, and take delight in honoring each other.

Romans 12:10

Bug and Honey Sandwiches

"Stop doing bad things! Turn to God!" a loud voice shouted. People walking along the road or working in the nearby fields, stopped and looked around.

"Did you hear something?" they asked each other. A few minutes later the voice rang out again, "Why are you just pretending to know God? Do you really think that you're fooling him?"

When the man who belonged to the voice stepped out into the light, a rumble of questions rolled through the crowd. "What is that he is wearing?" "It looks like . . . camel skin." "Whew! I bet he hasn't had a bath in weeks!" "Do you think he has ever cut his hair?" John ignored the whispered comments and went right on preaching.

"Why are you yelling at us? We don't need to worry about
this stuff. Our great-great granddaddy, was Abraham, a
famous man of God . . . or is it great-great-great granddaddy?
I forget. Anyway, we come from a good line. We're all set with
God, so go on and do your preaching somewhere else," the
man gave John a little shove that sent him on down the road.

"Wait a minute," another man said. "I've heard of you. You're John the Baptist. You live out in the wilderness by yourself. Your clothes are made of camel skins and you eat bugs and honey. (When he said that, some of the women got sick to their stomachs.) Some people say that you're the one the prophet Isaiah wrote about. They say that you're getting people ready to meet the Messiah." By this time a big crowd was gathered around John.

"Yes, I baptize people with water, which shows that they are turning away from their sins. But, the Messiah is coming soon and he will baptize people with the Holy Spirit. He will separate good people from bad people. He knows the difference. Be ready!" With that, John walked away, preaching his message of warning to any and all who would listen.

Based on Luke 3:1-20

Becoming a Man of God
A man of God tells about Jesus.

Way back before John the Baptist was even born, an angel told his parents that his job would be to tell people that Jesus was coming. He spent his life telling people that Jesus, the Savior, was coming. When people believed his message, he baptized them in a river to show that they were turning away from their sins and deciding to live for God. John knew what his job was and he gave his life to that work. He knew that people were sinners and he told them so—right to their faces.

How can you tell people about Jesus? Do you have to wear camel-skin clothes and eat bugs to be Jesus' worker? Of course not, the way you live your life and the way you treat people every day shows them what God's love is like. You also can invite friends to come to church, Sunday school, club or special programs with you where they can hear that God loves them.

Dad's Turn

John the Baptist didn't pull any punches. People were sinning and he told them so. Christians continue to do that today by being different—not weird—but different in our approach and attitudes to situations that life presents.

The story of John the Baptist is a good time to explain to your son how all members of God's family work together to share the news of God's love with the world. Some people are good at preaching, some are good at music, some are good at being friends, or helping out people with problems. Share with your son the way you feel God uses you to tell people about him. For example, you may be a good mechanic, so your personal ministry is that of fixing cars and showing people Christian love in action.

Help your son see ways that he can share God's love with his friends. Explain to him how he can stand up for what is right when others are doing something wrong. Help him to realize the ways he shares God's love. Reinforce his kind treatment of others and his sensitive heart.

A Verse to Remember

You are the light of the world—like a city on a mountain, glowing in the night for all to see.

Matthew 5:14

Miracle Lunch

"Momma, my friends are going to hear Jesus teach. Can I go? Please, Momma, can I go?" the little boy pleaded.

His mother considered the question for a minute, after all, her son wasn't very old. "Well, I guess so, but be sure to stay with the group. I'll pack a little lunch for you."

"That's OK, I don't need a lunch," the boy headed out the door.

"Right. You're always starving and you don't need a lunch. It will take me five minutes."

"There are a zillion people here," the boy said, picking his way through the crowd that was gathered to hear Jesus. Everyone sat quietly for hours listening to Jesus teach about God. The sun was low in the sky when one of Jesus' helpers interrupted him, "Master, it's late. Send these people home for dinner."

The little boy looked around in surprise. It didn't feel like he had been sitting for hours! He didn't want Jesus to stop teaching! So, when he heard Jesus say, "No, you give them dinner," he was thrilled.

"How can we give them dinner? We have no food and no money," the man argued.

"Umm, sir," the little boy shyly spoke up, "you can have my lunch. It's not very big, but, umm, if you want it . . ." his voice faded out.

Jesus' helper frowned at the little boy, "That won't do any good with all these people!" The boy sat down, embarrassed for even thinking that his little lunch could help. His buddies giggled and pointed at him.

A tear rolled down the boy's cheek, as a gentle hand slowly lifted his chin. Jesus looked right into his eyes, "Thanks for sharing your lunch." He took it, and lifted it up high, "Thank you, God, for this food," he prayed.

Then he broke the bread and fish into pieces and gave it to the disciples to pass out to the people. They kept coming back and getting more and more food from Jesus. "How is he getting so much food from my little lunch of 5 loaves of bread and 2 fish?" the boy wondered.

"Buuurrrp! No, thanks," the boy passed on a fourth helping. He couldn't eat another bite. More than 5000 people had all they wanted to eat, then Jesus' helpers picked up twelve baskets of leftovers. "That was awesome!" the boy thought. He glanced over at Jesus . . . who was smiling at him! "Wow! Just 'cause I shared my lunch. I got to help with a miracle!"

Based on John 6:1-13

Becoming a Man of God

A man of God shares what he has.

Wow! Do you think this little boy was brave? Would it have been a little scary to go up to Jesus' helper and offer his lunch? Besides, after he thought about it for a few minutes, he might have realized that he was pretty hungry, too. He could have ended up wishing that he hadn't given his lunch away. But, this little boy was willing to give the little bit that he had, if it would help someone else. That's Christian love in action—caring about others more than yourself.

Has someone ever shared something with you when you really needed it? What was it? How did you feel about that person? When was a time that you shared what you had with someone else? Did you feel good about sharing?

Dad's Turn

If you grew up with brothers and sisters, you may have some great sharing/not sharing stories from your childhood. Tell your son a story of when someone shared something special with you. How did you feel about that person afterwards? Recall a story when someone didn't share with you and tell your son how you felt at that time.

Talk with your son about what sharing means. Help him see that sharing time and energy is as important as sharing part of a cookie or candy bar. Explain to him that another way of sharing is through gifts and offerings to missionaries or church programs. Help him see the bigger business of sharing over the squabbles that young siblings or playmates might have over toys.

A Verse to Remember

Do for others what you would like them to do for you.

Matthew 7:12

A Happy Ending

"O God, please help my son get well. I know you gave him to me and he is so special to me. He's been sick a long time and no matter what I do he just seems to get worse. Please, God, since my husband died, this boy is all the family I have." The worried mother rocked her son, put cool rags on his feverish forehead, and prayed for all she was worth.

Even though the mother did everything she could think of, the boy died. With her heart aching, the woman sat beside her dead son's bed, holding his limp hand. She remembered how he used to run and laugh and play with his friends.

Friends brought food and flowers to her, but the sad momma didn't seem to notice. She just sat and stared at her son's body. Finally, her friends began making funeral arrangements. They thought the woman would sit beside her dead son forever if they didn't take charge.

On the day of the funeral one of her friends actually took the
woman's hand and led her out of the house. Other friends
lifted the boy's coffin to their shoulders and family and
friends followed along behind them to go bury the boy. The
sad little parade walked through town as people on the street
and in the shops watched them pass, feeling sorry for the sad
mother.

At the city gate, the funeral procession had to wait while people came into town. A group of men stepped aside to let the funeral pass. "It isn't hard to tell who the mother of the dead boy is," the men thought. Her body was so filled with grief that she could barely walk. Suddenly one of the men stepped up to the woman and took her hand. "Don't be sad," he said softly. The people who heard thought he was crazy. How could he say that when she had just lost her only son?

His words made sense when the man stepped up to the coffin and took the dead boy's hand. "Get up," he said. To everyone's amazement, the dead boy sat up! "Who is that guy?" people began asking each other.

"It's Jesus, the teacher from Nazareth," someone said. Jesus took the woman's hand and gently placed the boy's hand in it. He smiled at the joy in her face and laughed out loud when she pulled her alive-again-son into her arms, hugging him for all she was worth.

Based on Luke 7:11-17

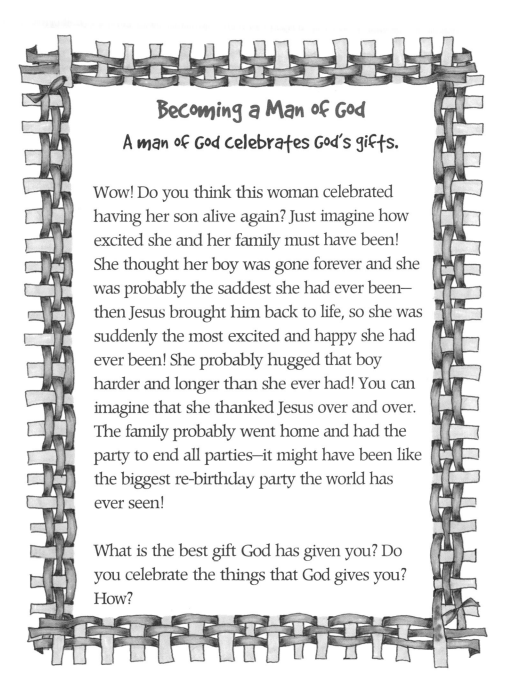

Becoming a Man of God
A man of God celebrates God's gifts.

Wow! Do you think this woman celebrated having her son alive again? Just imagine how excited she and her family must have been! She thought her boy was gone forever and she was probably the saddest she had ever been—then Jesus brought him back to life, so she was suddenly the most excited and happy she had ever been! She probably hugged that boy harder and longer than she ever had! You can imagine that she thanked Jesus over and over. The family probably went home and had the party to end all parties—it might have been like the biggest re-birthday party the world has ever seen!

What is the best gift God has given you? Do you celebrate the things that God gives you? How?

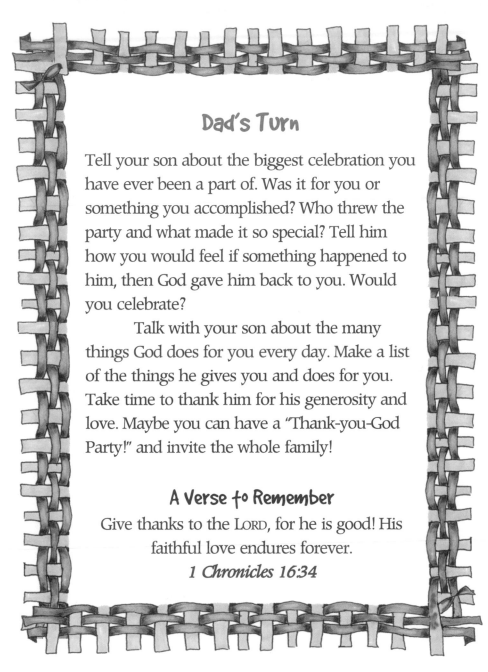

Dad's Turn

Tell your son about the biggest celebration you have ever been a part of. Was it for you or something you accomplished? Who threw the party and what made it so special? Tell him how you would feel if something happened to him, then God gave him back to you. Would you celebrate?

Talk with your son about the many things God does for you every day. Make a list of the things he gives you and does for you. Take time to thank him for his generosity and love. Maybe you can have a "Thank-you-God Party!" and invite the whole family!

A Verse to Remember

Give thanks to the LORD, for he is good! His faithful love endures forever.

1 Chronicles 16:34

The Short Storm

"Look at how the people listen so carefully to Jesus when he teaches," Peter whispered to John.

"Yeah, they want to hear every word he says," John whispered back. "But you know what? I'm tired and hungry. I wish he would stop so we could go get some dinner."

"Me, too. He's been teaching for hours. I don't know how he does it—he must be tired and hungry, too," Peter stretched and yawned.

When Jesus did finish teaching, the disciples started toward town to get dinner. But, Jesus stopped them, "Let's sail across the lake," he said.

"I was kind of hoping we could get some dinner first," someone said.

"Shh," Peter said, "you know it's best to do what Jesus says." So, without another word the disciples climbed into the boat and raised the sail. Jesus sat down and went right to sleep.

About half way across the lake the wind picked up and began bouncing the little boat up and down, blowing it sideways and splashing water into it.

"Lower the sail!"

"We're taking on water—start bailing!"

The disciples grabbed whatever they could find to scoop out water, but more and more water filled the boat. "We're going under! Help! JESUS! HELP!"

Someone ran to Jesus and shook his him. "Wake up, we're going to drown. Help us!"

Jesus stood up and looked out at the stormy waters. "Be quiet!" he shouted. Instantly the sea calmed down, the wind stopped blowing and the rain stopped. Everything was peaceful and quiet

"Wow! That was awesome." "Incredible!" "How did he do that?" the disciples whispered to one another.

Jesus looked around at his friends. "Where is your faith?" he asked. He was sad that they still didn't really believe he was the Son of God.

Jesus sat down and dozed off again. But, the disciples were too amazed to sit or sleep. "Who is he? How come the wind and waves do what he tells them to do?" they asked each other.

Based on Luke 8:22-25

Becoming a Man of God
A man of God learns from what he sees.

How many times had these very same disciples seen Jesus do miracles? How many times had they heard him teach about God? They knew he was the Son of God. But, when it came down to actually trusting their own lives to him, well, they had trouble with that. It seems like each time they saw Jesus do a miracle, they were able to believe a little more deeply that he was actually the Son of God. Each time they saw him do something miraculous, they asked each other who he was . . . each time the answer was the same—he is the Son of God, the Savior of the world. Seems like it should have been easier, doesn't it?

How do you feel about Jesus when you read about miracles like this one? How do you see his power in the world around you? When you recognize his power, does it help you believe who he is?

Dad's Turn

Can you recall the first time you saw an awesome display of God's power? Was it in a lightning storm? A volcano eruption? The birth of a child? Or perhaps you actually saw a miraculous healing or something of that sort. Tell your son about this experience.

Explain to your son how valuable the Word of God is to us. The stories recorded in it show Jesus' power and the miracles he did for people. By reading these stories we can learn what he is like and how he will take care of us.

Talk with your son about the ways he sees God's power. Ask him if it helps him to trust God more when he sees these displays of God's power.

A Verse to Remember

You are great and perform great miracles. You alone are God.

Psalm 86:10

Real kindness

The road to Jericho was usually crowded with travelers, so it was a little unusual that the businessman began his trip to Jericho alone. He didn't mind, though. The sun was shining, birds were singing and it was a lovely day. He enjoyed the walk and it didn't even seem odd that the road was empty. Until . . . some robbers jumped out from behind a rock and bonked him on the head. No one was around to stop them, so they took everything the man had . . . even his shoes and clothes, and left him on the road to die.

When the poor man woke up, he hurt all over and his clothes were covered with blood. "Those creeps just left me here to die. Ohhhh, it hurts to move. This isn't good, what am I going to do?" When he heard footsteps later, he struggled to lift his head, "Thank goodness . . . a priest. If anyone will help me, a priest will!"

But, to his surprise, the priest looked at him with disgust, "Ugh! Why is this piece of garbage lying in my way?" Then, he crossed the road and kept on walking.

The sun beat down on the poor man. "I'm so hot and thirsty. I wonder if anyone is ever going to help me?" He was about to give up hope when, once again he heard footsteps. This time he couldn't even lift his head, but when a temple worker leaned over him, he thought for sure he was saved! The temple worker poked him with his toe, "Hmm, you're beaten up pretty badly," he said, "you probably need help, but I've got work to do and important meetings this afternoon. I don't have time to help you," and with that he stepped over the man and kept on walking.

Now it was nearly dark. The poor man had been lying on the road all day. "I guess noone is going to help me, I'm going to die here. My poor wife and children," he thought. Then, he heard footsteps again, but he was too weak to even open his eyes until he felt a hand lift his head and gently pour a few drops of water into his dry mouth. "It's a Samaritan. They hate us Jews," he thought. "Well, if you're planning to rob me, you're too late. I've got nothing left!" He closed his eyes and waited to die.

He must have passed out because when the man opened his eyes again, he was lying in a soft bed in a nice inn. The Samaritan was cleaning his cuts and putting bandages on them. Then, he saw the good Samaritan pay the innkeeper gold coins to take care of him. The man sighed and let himself relax at last. He didn't have to worry now. He was going to be okay.

Jesus told this story to help people think about who they should be helping.

Based on Luke 10:30-37

Becoming a Man of God
A man of God doesn't play favorites.

The priest and temple worker in this story didn't show the love of God to the hurt man, did they? They didn't act like they cared about other people at all. Maybe they only took time to help people they felt were important. Showing God's love means being kind and helpful to all people—not just those who are like us or who we feel might be important people.

Do you know people who are different from you? Perhaps their skin is a different color or they speak a different language. Some people are different because they are poorer or richer than you. Are you tempted to treat these people differently than you treat your friends? If people who are different from you needed help, would it be easy for you to help them?

Dad's Turn

In your experiences in school or at work, are you around people who are of a different nationality, or are different from you in another way? Have you ever had an opportunity to befriend or help someone who may have been perceived as an "enemy"? Tell your son about this experience. Did you take a chance on this person and discover a new friend? Were you able to show an example of God's love to this person? How did you feel about your choice of behavior?

Does your son know people of different races, cultures, or from family situations different from yours? Talk about how he feels about them and how he treats them. Pray for these people and for opportunities to get to know them.

A Verse to remember

Live a life filled with love for others, following the example of Christ, who loved you and gave himself as a sacrifice to take away your sins.

Ephesians 5:2

Out for a Stroll

"Another storm. Why are there so many storms on this sea?" Peter mumbled, as he bailed water out of the boat again. A big wave crashed into Peter, knocking him to his knees. He sat for a minute looking out over the stormy sea. "Hey, what is that out there?" he asked.

"Quit loafing, we need your help bailing water," John answered.

"No really, it looks like . . . you're going to think I'm nuts . . . like someone walking on top of the water!" Peter pointed.

John looked where Peter was pointing. He shivered a little and said, "I wish Jesus was here. I always feel better when Jesus is with us."

"Yeah, me too. Besides that 'ghost' out on the water, this storm is getting pretty bad. I hope our boat doesn't take on much more water."

"Oh wow. Your 'ghost' on the water is getting closer. This is too weird," John stepped behind Peter's broad back.

Peter's eyes were as big as saucers as he watched the figure move toward their boat. "O God, help us, protect us!" he prayed.

"Peter, what are you afraid of? It's just me," Jesus almost sounded like he was teasing Peter. The big fisherman peeked open one eye and saw Jesus, walking on top of the stormy water.

"Jesus, is that you? Really? If it is, then let me come to you on top of the water!" Peter was climbing out of the boat as he shouted.

"Come on," Jesus called.

Peter leaped into the water and began running . . . almost skipping . . . across the stormy waves. He peeked back over his shoulder to see what the other disciples thought of him now. But, when he took his eyes off Jesus, he sank into the water like he had weights tied to his feet. "H-e-l-p M-e!" he gurgled. That's all he could get out before his mouth filled with water.

A gentle hand firmly grabbed Peter's hair and pulled his head out of the water. While Peter coughed and sputtered, Jesus said, "You don't have much faith, do you?"

The other disciples helped Peter climb back into the boat and wrap up in a blanket. Jesus got in the boat, too. Suddenly the wind stopped whirling. Stars glittered brightly in the sky, shining on a quiet sea.

It was amazing. Every eye was on Jesus' face as the men dropped to their knees in worship. "This man is truly the Son of God," one man whispered.

Based on Matthew 14:22-33

Becoming a Man of God
A man of God keeps his eyes on Jesus.

When Peter realized that it was Jesus walking on the water, he leaped out of the boat to join him. Peter didn't let much hold him back. He would try pretty much anything. His faith was exciting and bold. Peter did fine walking on top of the water through a big storm with waves crashing all around him and the wind blowing . . . until he took his eyes off Jesus. The key was that he looked back to see what the other disciples thought of him. He should have only cared what Jesus thought. When people get caught up in worrying about what other people think, they stop caring about what God thinks.

Do you care more about what your friends think about you or what God thinks of you?

Dad's Turn

Share a story with your son about a time when you got caught up in worrying about what people thought of you. Did this struggle with peer pressure weaken your relationship with God? How did you feel about yourself? Talk with your son about peer pressure and the danger of caring too much what other people think of you.

Remind your son that we should make every effort to keep our eyes on Jesus and keep our relationship with him as strong and healthy as possible. How do we do that? We stay close to him by reading his word and talking to him every day.

A Verse to Remember

Choose today whom you will serve . . . . But as for me and my family, we will serve the LORD.

Joshua 24:15

Courageous Investments

"Hey you, the master wants to see you," the foreman tapped a servant on the back. "You, too . . . and you over there." He singled three servants out of the dozens who were working together.

"What did we do? Are we in trouble?" the three servants smoothed their hair and clothes as they made their way into the master's grand house.

When the master came into the room, all three servants dropped to their knees. "I'm going away. While I'm gone, I want you to take care of my money," he said. He clapped his hands and a man appeared with a tray that held eight bags of gold. "Stand up," the master said to the first servant. "Here are five bags of my gold. I'm trusting you with it," he said, shaking the man's hand. "You're next," he said, pulling the second man to his feet. "I'm giving you two bags of gold." Turning to the third man, he said, "This last bag is for you. I want each of you to invest my money. Take care not to lose it." Then the master left.

Right away the first man invested the five bags of gold.
Before very long he had doubled the master's money. The
second man also went right to work and before the master
returned, he had four bags of gold. But, the third man
couldn't quite decide what to do with his one bag of gold.
Finally, he took it outside, dug a deep hole and buried it
under a bush.

A long time later the master returned home. "Well, what have you done with my money?" he asked.

"I invested the five bags of gold and now I have ten bags," the first servant announced, dropping the gold at his master's feet and backing away.

"Good job. You are a good servant," the master said.

"I invested my two bags and now I have four," the second man said.

"Good job. You are a good servant," the master said.

Do the best with what you've been given

The third servant nervously stepped forward, "Well, I was afraid because you sometimes get very angry. So I buried the gold you gave me and kept it safe!" he said.

"You didn't invest it? You didn't even put it in the bank to earn interest?" the master couldn't believe what he was hearing. "Take the gold from this man and give it to the one who has ten bags. If you don't do the best with what you've been given, then what you do have will be taken away!"

Based on Matthew 25:14-30

Becoming a Man of God
A man of God is a good steward.

When the master gave his money to the three servants and told them to take care of it, he didn't mean they should hide it and give him back the very same amount. He wanted them to take what he gave them and do something with it so they could give more back to him. Each of the three servants had a chance to be good stewards . . . that means they had a chance to do something with the master's money. He was pleased with the two who did that, but he wasn't happy with the one who just buried the money and gave him back the very same amount.

God gives each of his children gifts and talents. If he gives a talent for music, he is pleased if that person takes music lessons to become a better musician. Whatever the talent or gift that is given, it's good to learn to be better at doing it and then to share it with other people.

What gifts or talents has God given you? Do you like to sing or play a musical instrument? Are you good at making people laugh, or are you especially kind to others? How can you get better at using your gift?

Dad's Turn

Tell your son how you have worked to develop talents you have. When you were a child taking music lessons or going to sports camps, did you always enjoy that? Help him to see that improving yourself is sometimes work, but the end result is worth it.

Discuss with your son being a good steward with money, too. Tell him how you try to be wise when making purchases. Explain that you look for the best price on an object so that you get the most for your money. Help him understand that being a good steward is why you can't buy everything he wants.

Tell him about someone whose talents you admire—a musician, speaker, artist, athlete. How does that person share their gift with others? Do you think that person has worked hard to develop their gift?

A Verse to Remember

To those who use well what they are given, even more will be given, and they will have an abundance.

Matthew 25:29

Party Time!

"What are you so happy about? You walk around whistling like you actually enjoy being stuck on this farm!" the young boy shouted at his older brother.

"Quit complaining and get busy. We have a lot of fenceline to mend today," the older brother shook his head and kept right on working.

"Well, you can stay on this farm 'til you rot. I'm outta here. I've had all I can take of mucking out stalls and mending fences."

That very night the young son went to his dad, "I want more out of life than this farm. Give me my inheritance now. I'm going to the big city and live it up!"

His father sadly gave him the money and watched his young son leave. As soon as the boy got into the city, he lived the high life. Parties! Restaurants! Gifts for his friends! Soon, every cent his dad had given him was gone . . . and so were all his "friends."

"This stinks. I left home to get away from farm animals. Now the only job I can find is feeding pigs, and they have more to eat than I do! I guess the only thing to do is crawl back to Dad and ask for a job on his farm. I sure don't deserve to be treated like his son anymore," the boy sadly thought.

He headed for home, practicing what he would say to his dad the whole way. But, his dad saw him coming when he was still a long way off. "Yahoo! My boy is home!" he shouted, running to hug his son. The boy tried to give the speech he had practiced, but his dad kept hugging him.

"Make a big dinner. Put a purple robe and gold ring on the boy. My son is home so we'll party all night!" the old man had never been so happy!

Meanwhile, the older son was working away. "Is that music coming from the house?" he wondered. "What in the world is going on?"

Just then a servant ran up to tell him about the party. "What? I've been doing my work AND his while he's been off in the city wasting money. Now Dad is throwing him a party? Forget it. There's no way I'm going!"

When his older son didn't come up to the house, his dad came looking for him. "Son, don't you understand how I feel? I thought your brother was dead, but now he's here—alive and well. He is home so I have to celebrate."

Jesus told this story to show how God forgives us for doing wrong things and welcomes us back to him.

Based on Luke 15:11-32

Becoming a Man of God
A man of God is forgiven.

This young man was mixed up on what is really important, wasn't he? He wanted to party and have fun without working for money. But, when the money his dad gave him was gone, he couldn't even pay for food. It must have made his dad very sad when the young boy left home because the dad would miss him and he knew the boy was making a bad choice. Even though the boy wasted all the money, his dad forgave him and welcomed him home. The boy was so ashamed of his behavior that he was only going to ask his dad for a job, but his dad forgave him and threw a big party to welcome back his son.

      This is a good example of how God forgives us for the wrong things we do. When we tell him we're sorry for the things we have done, he forgives us and welcomes us back with joy and celebrating.

Have you ever told God that you are sorry for bad things you have done. Things such as being mean or selfish to your family or friends? Tell him, and then thank him for forgiving you!

Dad's Turn

Have you ever experienced real forgiveness from another person? Tell your son about a time you made a mistake or behaved badly and the person you wronged forgave you, with no strings attached. If this story involves your father, that's even better. How did you feel after being forgiven? How did you feel about the person who forgave you?

Explain the gift of salvation. Explain how the Lord Jesus Christ loves us so much that he came to earth and died for our sins. Because of that, God forgives our sins if we ask and he loves us—no matter what!

Pray with your son, thanking God for his love and forgiveness.

A Verse to Remember

If we confess our sins to him, he is faithful and just to forgive us and to cleanse us from every wrong.
1 John 1:9

A Tale of Two Men

"Out of my way. Let me through. Don't you know who I am?" the Pharisee's fancy robes swished as he pushed his way through the crowd of people entering the Temple for prayer time. Most people stepped out of his way, after all, he was a religious leader–a very important man!

On the other hand, a tax collector tried to get through the crowd for his own prayer time. But, no one stepped aside to let him in. "Dishonest cheat," someone said, right out loud. "That guy stole my hard-earned money and called it taxes. Now I barely have enough money to buy food for my kids," another man whispered to a friend.

Inside the Temple, hundreds of people knelt in prayer. The Pharisee heard the rumble of voices as their prayers were offered up to God. Instead of kneeling and praying quietly as the others were doing, the Pharisee stood up tall and began to pray loudly, "Thank you God, that I am not a sinner like other people . . . especially that tax collector over there. I don't cheat or lie. I fast twice a week and I give money to your work. O God, you are so lucky to have a friend like me!"

The people praying nearby couldn't believe what the Pharisee was saying. "We are all sinners," one woman thought. "Everyone does bad things sometimes. Well, God knows his heart better than I do," she sighed, going on with her own prayers. Across the way, the tax collector finally found a spot to pray. When he knelt, all the nearby people moved away. No one wanted to be around him.

Imagine the surprise of the people around him when they heard his whispered prayers, "O God, please forgive my sins. Show mercy to me, O God." He pounded his hands against his chest because he felt sorry for the unkind and dishonest things he had done.

Jesus told this story to show the difference between proud people who don't admit when they do something wrong and people who know they are sinners.

Based on Luke 18:9-14

Becoming a Man of God
A man of God asks forgiveness for his sins.

The Pharisee thought he was better than other people.
Maybe he even thought that he didn't ever sin. If he
really knew the truth, he would have known that all
people are sinners and need to ask God's forgiveness.
Tax collectors were usually dishonest cheaters who took
more money than people actually owed for taxes. Tax
collectors didn't have many friends. The people around
him must have been surprised to hear this tax collector's
prayer because he was sorry for his sins. He knew that
he did wrong things and that he needed to ask God's
forgiveness. Even though he did wrong things, he was
on the right track because he admitted his sins and
asked forgiveness.

Do you ever do wrong things? Do you think that some
people never do wrong things? Have you asked God's
forgiveness for wrong things you have done?

Dad's Turn

Does your son think that you never do anything wrong or never make a mistake? He might have the impression that only children do wrong things and adults have their lives all together. Give him a general example of how adults still struggle with doing wrong things. Help him to understand that the Pharisee's attitude was completely wrong. Everyone sins and needs to ask God's forgiveness.

Pray with your son now. Both of you may want to ask God's forgiveness and for his help to stop doing the same wrong things over and over.

A Verse to Remember

If we claim we have not sinned, we are calling God a liar and showing that his word has no place in our hearts.

1 John 1:10

Bird's Eye View

"Get out of my way! Don't you know who I am? Move it!"
Zacchaeus tried to muscle his way through the crowd. But no
one paid any attention to the little guy. The fact that he was a
tax collector didn't help. No one wanted to do anything nice
for him, because he cheated people out of their hard-earned
money!

"He's coming!" a man called as he ran toward the crowd.
"Jesus is coming!" The crowd of people pushed closer to the
road. Zacchaeus found himself at the back of the group. He
wouldn't be able to see anything except people's backsides.
"I've got to do something. I want to see Jesus, too,"
Zacchaeus thought. Then, he had an idea. He climbed up the
big sycamore tree next to the road and scooted out to the
end of a big branch.

Zacchaeus clung to the branch as the crowd around Jesus passed right below him. He had a bird's eye view of the great teacher! When Jesus stopped and looked up at him Zacchaeus nearly fell off his branch. "Come down, Zacchaeus. I would like to come to your house," Jesus said.

"M-m-my house? He wants to come to my house?" Zacchaeus was amazed. He jumped down from the tree and proudly walked through the crowd of people who hated him.

The little tax collector wanted to be sure that everyone saw that Jesus wanted to come to HIS house. He felt very important. "Ha! The teacher didn't ask to come to any of your houses," he wanted to say right out loud.

"Why is Jesus going with that cheater?" people complained. "He doesn't deserve special attention from Jesus." The little man ignored the nasty comments as he opened the door to his fine house.

Jesus went inside and closed the door. The tax collector listened as Jesus talked about God's love for all people. He talked to Zacchaeus about the way he had been cheating people out of their hard-earned money. When he finished, Zacchaeus quietly said, "I'm sorry for the way I've lived. I promise to pay back the people I've cheated. In fact, I'll pay back four times more than I owe them. And, I'll give half of my money to the poor." Jesus smiled. He knew that Zacchaeus loved God now and would treat people fairly.

Based on Luke 19:1-10

Becoming a Man of God
A man of God makes things right.

Zacchaeus was kind of a creep. He cheated people out of the money they worked very hard to earn. They couldn't do anything about it because he worked for the government. That's why Zacchaeus didn't have any friends and no one cared whether or not he could see Jesus. No one would get out of his way.

But, when Jesus taught Zacchaeus about God and how God wanted him to live, Zacchaeus believed him. Then, Zacchaeus' heart changed and he wanted to be kind to other people. He didn't just decide that from that day on, he would be fair. He decided to pay back the people he had cheated—four times more than he had stolen from them. Jesus was pleased with Zacchaeus.

If you have been unkind or unfair with someone, how can you make things right with them?

Dad's Turn

Tell your son about a time when you were treated unfairly or felt you were cheated. How did you feel about the situation? How did you feel about the person who was unfair or who cheated you? If you had been given a chance to do something nice for that person, would you have done it?

Remind your son that people who don't go to church or read the Bible only know about God by the way God's people treat them. If God's people act with fairness, kindness and love, others will get a little idea of what God is like. If we learn that we have hurt another person, we should make it right, just as Zacchaeus did.

If your son is sometimes selfish or unkind, talk with him about that behavior and gently suggest that he make an effort to treat others better. Pray with him about the way you both treat others.

A Verse to Remember

Dear children, let us stop just saying we love each other; let us really show it by our actions.

1 John 3:18

Nursing Duty

"Martha, I'm so tired. We've been taking care of Lazarus day in and day out for weeks. Is he ever going to get better?" Mary dropped into a chair, tired and worried.

"I don't know," Martha sighed. "But, he's our brother. We have to do whatever we can to take care of him." She fluffed a pillow as she talked. Mary squeezed cool water from a cloth and put it on Lazarus' forehead.

Lazarus had been sick for quite a while. Martha tried all the home remedies she knew—everything their mother had done when they were children. But, Lazarus just got worse. She didn't know what else to do.

One afternoon Mary was shopping and someone mentioned that Jesus was staying in a nearby town. Mary ran all the way home, "Martha! Our friend Jesus is nearby. Let's send for him. I know he can help Lazarus!" They sent a message, asking Jesus to come right away.

"Where is he?" Mary asked out loud. "We sent the message to Jesus days ago. Why hasn't he come?" Martha just shook her head. She didn't have an answer for her sister. Meanwhile, Lazarus continued to get worse. Then, late one night, he quietly died.

"I don't understand. Jesus is our friend. He's even stayed in our home before. Why didn't he come?" Mary asked through her tears. Martha tried not to ask herself those same questions. She kept busy making funeral arrangements for her brother.

But the frustration and questions flooded her heart a few days later when someone said, "Jesus is coming!"

"Now? He comes now? Lazarus is dead and buried. What good can he do now? Why didn't he come when he could have helped my brother?" Martha spilled out her frustration to Jesus. Mary couldn't believe the way her prim and proper sister spoke to him. "The bottom line, Jesus, is if you had come, Lazarus wouldn't have died!" Martha shouted.

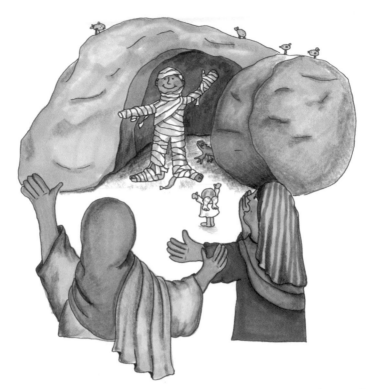

Jesus was sad at Martha's pain. "Where is Lazarus buried?" he asked. The sisters led him to the tomb, thinking that he wanted to pay his respects. Instead, Jesus called out, "Open the tomb!"

"No! Lazarus has been dead four days. He will smell terrible," Martha warned.

But Jesus called, "Lazarus, come out!" Mary hid her eyes but Martha held her breath and watched the tomb door.

"Mary, look," she whispered. Lazarus was standing in the tomb door—alive and well.

Based on John 11:1-44

Becoming a Man of God
A man of God is honest with God.

Martha didn't pull any punches. She told Jesus exactly how she felt, how disappointed she was that he hadn't come to help Lazarus. She knew that it was okay to be honest with him. He could take it. Besides, he knows how we feel in our hearts, so even if we say what we think is the "right thing to say", but we feel differently in our hearts, we aren't fooling him.

God made us with feelings and he knows that we're sometimes unhappy or disappointed. We can tell him exactly how we feel, and he will help us deal with our feelings.

Have you ever been disappointed when God didn't answer a prayer the way you wanted him to? Did you tell him how you felt? Are you generally honest with other people about how you feel?

Dad's Turn

Living a healthy Christian life means we are able to be honest with God. If we always say what we think is the "right thing" or we act like everything is just fine when we're actually struggling inside, then our relationship with God isn't based on truth.

This kind of dishonesty spills over into relationships with other people. That means we smooth over our feelings of hurt or disappointment with others, but carry the resentment deep in our hearts. Give your son an example of a time when you weren't honest about your feelings . . . with God or with someone else. Did you carry around resentment for a while? Did you finally deal with it?

Reinforce with your son that honesty must be accompanied with kindness. Tell him how pleased you are when he is honest and kind about his own feelings.

A Verse to Remember

Search me, O God, and know my heart, test me and know my thoughts.

Psalm 139:23

Dirty Coats, Palm Branches, and Noisy Rocks

"Peter, I don't have a good feeling about this," John whispered.

"Relax, will you? We're just doing what Jesus said to do. If he says it's OK, then it's gotta be OK," Peter whispered back. He untied the rope and started to lead the colt down the path.

"HEY YOU! Are you stealing my colt?" the angry man's face was so red that John thought he might have a heart attack. He ran toward them shaking his fist. "Leave my colt alone!" he shouted again.

"Jesus...use our coats for a saddle."

To John's amazement, Peter very calmly answered, "Sir, we're not stealing this colt, the Master needs it." Even more amazing, the man stopped complaining. He nodded his head, quietly turned around and went into his house. When they took the colt to Jesus, he started to climb onto it. "Wait," Peter cried. Taking off his coat, he spread it on the colt's back. "OK, now," he stepped aside so Jesus could get on the colt.

The disciples walked along behind the colt that Jesus was riding into Jerusalem. Word spread quickly that Jesus was coming and soon crowds of people lined the road. The disciples looked uneasily at each other as cries of "Hosanna! Bless the King who comes in the name of the Lord!" filled the air.

"What the . . ." Peter ducked as a palm branch smacked him in the face. "What are these people doing?" he wondered. Looking around he saw people waving palm branches in front of Jesus. Other people had spread their coats on the ground so the colt was stepping on them. They didn't even want Jesus' clothes to touch the ground.

"Psst, Peter, look over there," John whispered. Peter turned to see a group of Pharisees standing with their arms folded across their chests. These were not happy men. "Tell your followers to be quiet," one of them snapped at Jesus. In one smooth movement, all the disciples turned to look at Jesus. What would he say to the religious leaders?

"Sir," he quietly replied, "if they kept quiet, the stones along the road would burst into cheers." Slowly, the disciples' heads swiveled back to the Pharisees. But, they didn't say another word. Smart guys.

Based on Luke 19:28-40

Becoming a Man of God
A man of God can't help but praise him.

What an amazing sight! Jesus riding a donkey down streets lined with people shouting praises, waving palm branches and spreading their coats on the ground. The people couldn't stop shouting their praises. They couldn't seem to control themselves. They knew that Jesus was someone special.

When the Pharisees told Jesus to make the people be quiet, he knew that the rocks themselves would shout praises, because when God is present, praise just comes naturally. If the people were quiet, then nature itself would praise him!

How do you praise God? Do you sing? Shout praises? Draw pictures for him? Praise God for something right now!

Dad's Turn

What makes you shout with excitement? Do you get excited while watching sports and loudly cheer for your team? Talk with your son about situations where you get excited enough to shout and cheer.

If you have ever had an experience of being filled with praise and adoration for God to the point of not being able to keep silent, tell your son about it. Tell him how you praised God for that experience.

Remind your son that it is important to praise God for the wonderful things he does and not just always ask him to do things for you.

Ask your son what he would like to praise God for today. Help him do so, either through prayer or song, or making a picture of praise to God.

A Verse to Remember

Let everything that lives sing praises to the LORD!
Psalm 150:6

My Father's House

"Best deals in town! Get your sacrificial birds here! All your temple needs . . . right here!" The shouts could be heard throughout the usually quiet, respectful hush of the temple, offering the best deals and buys "too good to pass up!" The money-hungry salesmen even had signs hanging from the grand marble columns advertising their deals.

When Jesus came to pray in the temple, he couldn't believe what he saw! Pushing his way through the crowds, he got more and more angry at the salesmen who were stealing money from the worshipers. "Poor Jewish people come here to worship God, but these men are over-charging and stealing money from the worshipers. They are trying to get rich by people's worship!"

"This is not the way to treat God's house!" he continued. Walking up to one man's table, Jesus swung his arm across it, brushing coins and papers to the floor.

"Hey, what do you think you are doing?" the man shouted. Jesus ignored him and began pushing over tables and ripping down signs. Arms grabbed at him, trying to stop the destruction, but he kept right on clearing the temple.

"This is God's house—my father's house—and it is to be a place of prayer. It is not a place for you to make money by cheating people who come to worship God," Jesus worked his way up and down the aisles, turning over table after table, spilling money and scattering people as he went.

When the floor was covered with coins and birds were flapping all over the temple, the money changers took off running, afraid of what this crazy man might do next. But, Jesus was finished, he had made his point. He sat down and people quickly gathered around him. Some sat in awe, some begged for healing, some wanted him to bless their children. Shouts of, "Praise God for the Son of David!" echoed through the temple. The jealous Pharisees stood in a corner and made plans for ways to get rid of Jesus.

Based on Matthew 21:12-17

Becoming a Man of God
A man of God takes a stand against wrong.

Jesus didn't like it when people were cheated. He especially didn't like it when the poor people who came to worship God were cheated. He believed that the temple should not be a place where people came to make money, it was God's house where people came to worship. The people who sold animals to be used in sacrifices had started overcharging and cheating the poor people. Jesus had to stop this kind of behavior. He couldn't let it keep happening.

Have you ever seen something happening that you felt was wrong? Did you see people being mistreated, or cheated? Did you see someone being disrespectful of God's house? Did you do anything to stop the wrong behavior?

Dad's Turn

Have you ever gotten involved in a cause against something you felt was wrong? What was it? How did you get involved? What was the outcome? Were you frightened about getting involved? Did it feel good to have a part in changing something?

Talk with your son about the importance of keeping worship pure. It hurts our worship to be more concerned about making money than about serving God and learning more about him. Jesus wanted people everywhere to have the chance to worship God—not just those who could afford the prices the merchants were charging.

Ask your son if there is any "cause" that he would like to take a stand against. Talk about ways he could get involved and take a stand against something unfair or unjust.

A Verse to Remember

Obey me, and I will be your God and you will be my people.
Only do as I say, and all will be well.

Jeremiah 7:23

Broken Hearts, Broken Dreams

Jesus' friends stuck together, seeming to move around as a single unit. His brokenhearted mother, Mary, was in the middle of their group. As they watched soldiers beating him, Mary slumped slowly to the ground.

John caught her and another friend came over to help. She leaned against John and someone brought a cup of water, but she waved it away standing up again, straining to see Jesus.

A "crack!" rang through the air when a Roman soldier slapped a whip across Jesus' back. His friends hid their eyes, but not Mary, her eyes were glued to Jesus. "Get moving!" the soldier shouted. Jesus hoisted the wooden cross to his shoulder and plodded down the road. People lining the road shouted, "Hey, King of the Jews, why don't you call an army of angels to save you? Haa haa ha!" Mary had to look away now. It was just too hard to watch.

Mary and the others followed the crowd to a hill outside of town. The soldiers threw the cross to the ground and pushed Jesus down on top of it. They lifted big hammers and nailed Jesus' hands and feet into the wood. He groaned a low, agonizing moan when they dropped the heavy cross into the ground. Mary's heart broke, but the crowd cheered, "Come on King of the Jews . . . save yourself! Where's your miracle power now?"

People milled about, watching Jesus die, pointing at him, making fun of him. "How can they do this?" Jesus' friends asked one another, but Mary watched in silence. She had known Jesus from the minute he was born. She knew that he had never done anything bad or wrong or even unkind. But, the words of the angels that had spoken to her and Joseph before Jesus was born floated into her mind, "This baby is the Son of God, Savior of the world." Mary knew that was why this terrible thing was happening.

As the day wore on, some people got tired and went on back to town. Mary moved closer to the cross. She could sense John standing behind her. She looked into Jesus' eyes–the eyes of her son–God's Son. In spite of the terrible things that had been done to him, his eyes were filled with love, even for the people who were torturing him. John slipped his arm around Mary's shoulder when Jesus said, "It is finished."

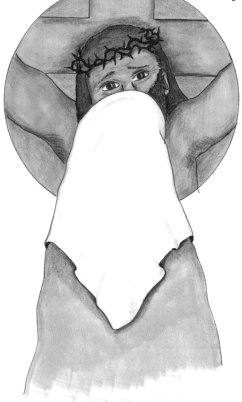

When he died, part of her died, too . . . and yet she knew that even though her son was dead, her Savior would live forever.

Based on John 19:16-30

Becoming a Man of God

A man of God knows that Jesus died for him.

The murder of Jesus was a terrible thing. One of the reasons Jesus came to earth was to make a way for people to be able to live in heaven with God. His death paid the price for our sins. Before Jesus died, people had to give sacrifices to God to pay for their sins, but Jesus' death ended that forever. Jesus could have called angels to rescue him and stop the crucifixion, but he loves us so much that he was willing to die for us.

Do you believe that Jesus died for YOUR sins? Have you thanked him for doing that?

Dad's Turn

Explain to your son that Jesus died for our sins, even though he had never sinned. That's how much he loved us. Explain that God loves people so much that he gave his only Son for our sins.

Can you share a time when you did all you could to protect your son from injury or pain, then explain how amazing it is that God willingly gave his Son.

Who explained the plan of salvation with you and prayed with you when you accepted Christ as your Savior? Share the plan of salvation with your son again. If he hasn't yet prayed to receive Christ, ask him if he wants to do so now.

Thank God together for his gift of sending Jesus to earth. Thank Christ for his death on the cross.

A Verse to Remember

Believe on the Lord Jesus and you will be saved.

Acts 16:31

Good News Morning

"It's hard to keep going when your hope is taken away," thought Mary. "I know I've done the things I'm supposed to do these past few days, but I honestly can't remember much about them." The sun was just coming up as Mary and two friends walked to the tomb where Jesus was buried. Hope died for Jesus' followers . . . when he died. He had taught them about God, and how to live for him. But, then he died and now some of them wondered if any of what he taught was true.

Even in the middle of their pain, the three women had to do what was right. Their custom said that Jesus' body must be covered with perfumes and oils, or his burial wouldn't be finished. They wanted to do the right thing so they were trudging to the tomb, even though their hearts were numb with pain.

The three women had been friends for years, shared happy times and hard times, but today, none of them knew what to say, so they walked in silence. But then, one of them remembered watching the soldiers roll a big stone over the opening to the tomb. "It took six soldiers to place that stone. How are we going to move it to get into the tomb?" she asked her friends.

"How much more do we have to go through?" her friend answered, dropping her basket of perfumes. "I just don't know how much more I can take," she sighed.

"Come on, we'll figure something out," Mary whispered. Heads bowed, they rounded the last curve in the road before reaching the tomb. Suddenly, the woman in front stopped, and her friends bumped right into her.

"It's . . . gone!" she whispered. "The stone is gone. What does that mean?" They held onto one another as fear rose in their hearts. "What was going on?"

The bravest of the three slowly
approached the open tomb.
Cautiously stepping inside, she
waited for her eyes to adjust to the
darkness. "You're looking for Jesus, but he's not here. He's alive.
He came back to life, just as he told you he would," the angel's
voice announced. Looking around, the woman saw that Jesus
WAS gone. "He's alive! He's alive!" she shouted to her friends.
"He has come back to life just as he said he would! Praise God!"

Based on Mark 16:1-7

Becoming a Man of God
A man of God celebrates!

This story is an example of how little Jesus' friends really understood him. He had told them he would come back to life—but that was too hard for them to believe. So, they were all heartbroken and lost when he died. All their hope was gone. These women going to the tomb were just doing what they did for anyone who died. They surely didn't expect that Jesus' body wouldn't be in the tomb. But, when the angel told them that Jesus was alive, they were filled with high-fiving-heart-skipping joy! HE WAS ALIVE! . . . HE IS ALIVE!

Celebrate this today—even if it's not Easter time! Thank God that Jesus is alive! Tell someone this good news!

Dad's Turn

What's the best news you ever received? Why did it make you so happy? How did you celebrate? Who was the first person you shared your happy news with?

Talk with your son about what Jesus' resurrection means to us. In all other religions, the person who was worshiped died . . . and stayed dead. Jesus came back to life (as he said he would) and he is living in heaven, watching over us, taking care of us, and still paying the price for our sins. Someday, he will come back to earth and get all Christians, taking us to heaven to live with him forever! Celebrate!

A Verse to Remember

Forgetting the past and looking forward to what lies ahead, I strain to reach the end of the race and receive the prize for which God, through Christ Jesus, is calling us up to heaven.

Philippians 3:13-14

Seeing Is Believing

"He's dead, all right? Just let it go. We saw the soldiers drag his body down from the cross and put him in the tomb. He's dead, so quit talking about some miraculous resurrection," Thomas stomped around the room shouting at his friends, even though they tried to shush him so the Pharisees wouldn't hear their argument.

"Thomas, just listen. Yes, we saw them put Jesus' body in the tomb. He was dead. We're not arguing that. But, the women went out on Sunday to take care of his body . . . and he was gone!" Peter told the story again, but Thomas kept stomping away. Peter grabbed his arm and pulled him back.

"And then the other day, some of us were in this very room. The door was locked, the windows were shut—that's the honest truth. All of a sudden, Jesus was standing here right in front of us! He talked to us. He said that he was sending the Holy Spirit to help us. He said we should forgive people's sins. It's the truth, Thomas!"

Thomas threw up his hands in disgust, "You're crazy! I tell you, HE IS DEAD! I will not believe what you're telling me unless I see him for myself. No, not just see him, I will have to touch the wounds on his body!" Thomas headed for the door, he had heard enough for one day.

About a week later the disciples were together again in that same locked room. Each man was lost in his own thoughts, when a familiar voice broke the silence, "Thomas. Touch the wounds in my hands and side. Believe."

"Jesus, it's really you. You are alive!" Thomas whispered, sliding off his chair and onto his knees.

"You believe because you can see me and touch me," Jesus said. "Think how special those are who haven't seen me, but believe anyway."

Based on John 20:19-29

Becoming a Man of God
A man of God has faith.

Thomas was one of Jesus' closest friends, one of the disciples who was with him when he healed sick people and brought dead people back to life. Thomas knew that Jesus could do miracles . . . he had seen it with his own eyes. But, he couldn't believe that Jesus was really alive. His faith just wasn't that strong. So, Jesus appeared to Thomas and he even let Thomas touch the scars on his hands from when he was nailed to the cross. Jesus was probably happy to do that, but he pointed out how special people are who believe in him without actually seeing and touching him. Having faith means you believe something is—even if you can't see it or touch it.

Would you be like Thomas and actually have to see Jesus before you believed he was alive? Or, would you believe based on the fact that other people had seen him?

Dad's Turn

Are you a "show me" kind of guy who doesn't easily believe things that you haven't seen for yourself? Tell your son about a time when you had to believe something by just having faith—without any physical or practical reason to believe. Was it hard? Were you later glad that you believed? Did this experience make it easier to have faith the next time?

Talk with your son about some examples of things you both believe in, even though you can't see them or explain them, such as the sun coming up every morning, or the stars and moon staying up in the sky. Discuss things you know to be true about God and explain to your son that since he believes those things, he already has some faith.

Ask God to help your faith grow stronger every day.

A Verse to Remember

You love him even though you have never seen him. Though you do not see him, you trust him, and even now you are happy with a glorious, inexpressible joy.

1 Peter 1:8

Chariot Race

"Philip, God wants you to go south down the road that goes from Jerusalem to Gaza," an angel said. Philip didn't even ask why. He turned right around and headed to Gaza. Philip had enough experience to know that when an angel of God tells you to do something, you do it with no questions asked. He had no idea why God wanted him to make this trip, but he always obeyed God.

As Philip hurried down the road, a fancy carriage came flying by and nearly knocked him off the road. A man from Ethiopia was riding inside. "He must be very important," Philip thought. The carriage was already a good ways down the road when the Holy Spirit said, "Philip, run along beside the carriage." Again, Philip asked no questions, he just broke into a full run—faster than he had ever run in his whole life. When he caught up with the carriage, he heard the man reading verses from the book of Isaiah.

"Do you understand what you're reading?" Philip called. The Ethiopian was surprised that a man was jogging along beside his chariot.

"How can I understand unless someone explains it to me. Do you understand it?"

"Yes, I can explain what it means," Philip answered. So, the man stopped the carriage and Philip climbed in.

"These verses are talking about Jesus of Nazareth," Philip explained. He mentioned other verses he knew, too. Verses that explained why Jesus came to earth and how he was killed, but came back to life and lives in heaven making a way for all who believe in him to come to heaven someday. Philip told the Ethiopian the whole story of God's wonderful love.

"Stop the carriage! Stop!" the man shouted. "Look, there's some water over there. Why can't I be baptized right now? I believe what you're telling me about Jesus."

Philip and the man went into the water and Philip baptized him. As he lifted the man out of the water, God took Philip away and the man never saw him again, but he praised God all the way back to Ethiopia.

Based on Acts 8:26-40

Becoming a Man of God
A man of God shares what he knows.

There are a few lessons in this story: Philip listened
when the Holy Spirit spoke to him and he obeyed
when he was told what to do. He was willing to share
what he knew with someone who appeared to be an
important government official—Philip wasn't scared of
him. Philip knew quite a bit about the Bible and about
God and he explained everything he understood to
the Ethiopian man. Since he was willing to tell the
man what he knew, the man accepted Jesus and
became a Christian! Philip must have been pretty
excited about that.

Have you ever been able to share what you know
about God with someone? Were you nervous to talk
about something so important? Was your friend
interested in hearing more about God?

Dad's Turn

Tell your son about a time when someone shared information with you. Maybe your dad or grandfather taught you carpentry, or how to throw a spiral football pass. Did you appreciate the person who taught you? Did you use the information? Has someone mentored you in your Christian walk, explaining deeper things about the Christian faith? Who? How do you feel about that person?

Talk with your son about some of the basic facts of the Christian faith. Let him explain his faith, in a way he understands. He can practice sharing this information with you, so when he has a chance to share with a friend, he will already be experienced. Pray together for opportunities for both of you to share your faith with others.

A Verse to Remember

You will receive power and will tell people about me everywhere.

Acts 1:8

Hate Turns to Love

"I hate Christians!" Saul stomped across the room, searching for the words to express his anger. He got a knot in his stomach every time he saw someone who claimed to follow the teachings of Jesus. "My mission in life is to get rid of Christians!" he announced one day. "I'll do whatever it takes!" The only thing that brought a smile to Saul's sour face was standing outside the jail and making fun of the Christians he had thrown in there.

"Well," Saul said brushing the dust from his hands, "I've taken care of all the Christians in Jerusalem. My work is done. Wait a minute, it's done here . . . but what about the other towns? Oh yeah, I've still got work to do!"

So, Saul and his buddies set off for Damascus. Pretty soon, Saul heard a voice, "Saul, why are you persecuting me?" He stopped and looked around, but didn't see anyone. His friends didn't seem to have heard the voice at all.

"Saul," the voice said again, "why are you persecuting me?"
This time a light shot down from the sky, directly onto Saul.
He dropped to the ground, blinded, and crawled on his hands
and knees, trying to get away from the light. But the light
moved along with him and the voice kept asking, "Why?
Why?"

Saul's know-it-all friends were speechless. They could
hear the voice, but they couldn't figure out where it was
coming from.

"Who are you?" Saul asked. Deep in his heart he already knew the answer.

"I'm Jesus, the one you're persecuting," the voice answered.

Saul hung his head, "It's true then. Jesus is real. The Christians have been right all along. I'm the one who has been wrong. Right there on the dusty road to Damascus, Saul told Jesus he was sorry for everything he had done.

At that very moment, Saul's heart was changed. He no longer wanted to hurt Christians, now he was a Christian, too. God changed Saul's name to Paul and from that moment on, Paul's life was devoted to telling people about about Jesus' love.

Based on Acts 9

Becoming a Man of God

A man of God changes when he hears the truth.

Saul wasn't a very nice guy. He didn't like Christians one little bit and he did whatever he could to make their lives miserable and to keep them from sharing their faith with other people. He didn't believe that Jesus was God's Son or that he rose from the dead . . . until this experience. Then, once Saul realized that it was Jesus talking to him, and that what he was saying was true, he changed completely, 100%! From that moment on, all his energy was spent on teaching about God and his Son, Jesus

What do you give a lot of your energy to? What do you get excited about being a part of?

Dad's Turn

Have you ever been passionately involved in a "cause"? What was it? How did you get involved? Did you ever view Christianity with sarcasm or even anger? What changed your attitude?

Have you seen changes in your son's attitudes and behavior as he has grown up some or has become more serious about living for God? Compliment him on the improvements in his behavior. Help your son make a list of people you know who may be antagonistic toward the truths of the Gospel. Begin praying for those people, asking God to speak to their hearts and soften their attitudes toward Christ.

A Verse to Remember

Draw close to God, and God will draw close to you.
James 4:8

Dreaming a Lesson

"Oh wow! I just had the weirdest dream!" Peter came
downstairs rubbing the sleep from his eyes. Simon, his host,
waited for Peter to explain. "This big sheet came down from
the sky and it was filled with all kinds of foods that we can't
eat. You know, foods that are unclean." Simon looked
confused so Peter explained, "It would be a sin to eat them!"
Now Simon got it.

"But then, this voice said, 'Eat this!' But I said, 'No way!' but the voice said, 'God says it's OK!' What do you think this means?" Peter asked. Simon just shook his head—he didn't have a clue!

At just about the same time, a Roman army officer named Cornelius was having a pretty weird dream of his own.

In Cornelius' dream an angel said, "God has seen your gifts to the poor. He knows you are a kind man. Send your servant to Joppa to find Peter. Have Peter come here and teach you about God." When Cornelius woke up, he did exactly what the angel had told him to do.

Peter was still trying to figure out what his dream meant when Cornelius' three servants knocked on the door. "What do you want?" he asked them.

"Our master is an officer in the Roman army. He wants you to come back with us and teach him about God."

"Well, it's kind of late. Why don't you stay overnight here and we'll go tomorrow," Peter answered.

When Peter got to Cornelius' house, he was surprised to see that Cornelius had invited many friends and relatives to hear what he would teach them. "According to Jewish law, I shouldn't even be here," Peter said right away. "The law says that a Jew shouldn't come into the house of someone who isn't Jewish. But, God taught me an important lesson in a dream the other day. He taught me that when he says something is OK, then I should believe him. So, if he wants you to know about him, I shouldn't refuse to teach you, just because you're not Jewish." Then Peter taught them many things about God.

Based on Acts 10

Becoming a Man of God

A man of God has an open mind and heart.

The Jewish people lived by pretty strict rules stating what they could and could not do. God spoke to Peter in this dream and basically said, "Lighten up!" God loves all people. He wanted Peter to teach about God's love, even to people who weren't Jewish.

Some people today live by pretty strict rules, too. They only want to be around people who think like they do, dress like they do, speak the same language—but if we all felt like that, some people would never hear about God's love!

Do you know any kids who speak a different language than you, or are from another country? Do they have different beliefs or customs? Are you uncomfortable being around them? How can you be friendlier to them?

Dad's Turn

Have you ever encountered prejudice? Was it toward you, or did you observe it toward someone else? How did you feel about it? Did you do anything to stop it or try to change people's attitudes?

As you have grown up have you encountered rigid rules about how to live the Christian life? How did these affect your own Christian growth?

Talk with your son about rules—some are good and made for our safety and protection. Sometimes rules are made because people are afraid to be around those who are different or are afraid of change.

Talk to your son about people in your neighborhood or town who are not necessarily like you. How can you befriend them? How can you help others to be open to getting to know these people? Remind him that only by becoming their friends will you have chances to share God's love with them.

A Verse to Remember

Love each other. Just as I have loved you, you should love each other.

John 13:34

Prison Break!

"Can't you take these chains off so I can sleep?" Peter asked. But, his guards didn't even answer. After all, they were chained to him, so they were going to have trouble sleeping, too. With a guard on each side of him, Peter leaned back against the prison's stone wall. But one guard snored so loud that neither Peter or the other guard had any hope of getting any rest. Peter sighed, and settled down to watch bugs crawl around the floor.

"Why am I in prison anyway?" Peter thought. "I didn't do anything except teach people about Jesus. Why is that so bad?" Even as he thought that, Peter remembered his friend, James. King Herod murdered him because of his faith . . . and people laughed and cheered that murder! "I wonder what the king plans to do with me?" Peter was a little nervous. "I've got to get some sleep," he tried to shake the anxious thoughts from his mind. He rolled the snoring guard onto his side, trying to shut him up. That made the chain cut into his leg, but it was better than the snoring.

It was very late when Peter finally fell asleep. He had nightmares about what might happen to him. Since there were 4 squads of 4 soldiers standing guard outside his cell he knew that King Herod wanted to be sure he didn't escape.

Peter's sleep was restless. He tried to toss and turn, but the chains wouldn't let him. Right in the middle of his nightmare a bright light shone into his cell. It was brighter than anything he had ever seen.

Something stuck him in the ribs, and Peter opened his eyes. "Is it morning already?" he moaned. "Wait a minute the guards are still sleeping, so I must be dreaming." Then he saw a shining angel standing in front of him.

"Get up and get dressed," the angel said. Peter shook his chained arms. "How am I supposed to move?" he started to ask. But before he could say a word, the chains fell off his arms and legs. The angel motioned for Peter to follow him through the prison, past the sleeping guards, and out the door. Soon Peter was standing on the street outside the prison.

"How can I ever thank . . ." Peter turned to say, but, the angel was gone! Now Peter knew for sure that he wasn't dreaming.

He hurried to see his friends, who were praying for him. At first the servant who answered the door was so shocked that she forgot to open it for him. "Hey, let me in," Peter pounded on the door. When she opened the door, Peter rushed in and told everyone how God had saved him from prison and whatever King Herod had planned for him.

Based on Acts 12:1-19

Becoming a Man of God
A man of God is saved by God.

Peter was in jail because he was a Christian—not a very popular thing to be. His only crime was teaching about Jesus. He knew that some other Christians had been put in jail, and not treated very well—James was killed—and the people laughed! We don't know if Peter was frightened or if he came close to giving up hope. However, we do know that God sent the angel to lead him out of prison. God saved Peter from whatever King Herod had planned. Peter trusted God enough to obey the angel and follow it out of prison.

God takes care of his children. He often saves us from problems—not always with a big show like sending an angel, but every day he protects his children from danger or problems.

Thank God for his salvation and protection in your life.

Dad's Turn

Tell your son about a time you were rescued or protected from danger by someone. How did you feel? Were you frightened? Now tell him about ways you have protected him from danger or problems. Tell him you love him and are constantly concerned for his safety and well being.

Thank God for his love and protection for both of you. Thank God for providing a way of salvation for his children.

A Verse to Remember

The LORD keeps watch over you as you come and go, both now and forever.

Psalm 121:8

Prison Unescape

The jailer shoved Paul into a dark cell in the very center of the prison. Roaches and spiders scurried across the floor. Paul had been in prison before, but this time he knew that he and Silas were in big trouble. The jailer was given strict orders to keep them from escaping!

"So much commotion, and all I did was try to free a young girl from the demon that was controlling her. You'd think people would thank me for that, but no . . . I'm in prison for it!" Sometimes people's reactions confused Paul. When the soldiers grabbed him and Silas and beat them, it reminded Paul of his earlier life, when he beat Christians and threw them into jail—just because they were Christians.

"Praise God"

Paul and Silas settled down on the floor with their feet chained together. Paul reminded Silas of something important, "We can tell the other prisoners here how much God loves them. Even if we can't see them face to face, we can sing praises with all our hearts!"

"Let's do it," Silas agreed. They sang, slightly off key, but full of joy.

"Those guys are crazy," the other prisoners thought at first. But, then they listened to what Paul and Silas were singing about. Every single prisoner listened and thought about God's love.

Leaning back against the cold walls, many prisoners thought about God for the first time in years. Around midnight the walls and floor of the prison started shaking a little, then harder and harder. Paul and Silas held onto each other. The floor bounced and jerked and the chains holding them broke like paper. The prison door broke off–the earthquake was setting every prisoner free. Some men dashed out the door, ready to grab this ticket to freedom.

"Stop!" Paul shouted. "All of you wait!" When the jailer heard about the earthquake, he thought, "My prisoners have escaped. I will be executed!" He took out his sword and started to kill himself, then he heard Paul shout, "Don't hurt yourself. We're all here!"

"You stayed here, even knowing that you might be killed?" The jailer was very impressed. "How do I become a Christian?" he wanted to know. Paul was happy to explain that!

Based on Acts 16:16-40

Becoming a Man of God
A man of God doesn't take the easy way out.

Paul and Silas could have run out of the jail, just like the other prisoners were going to do. That would have been an easy ticket to freedom. But, that's not the kind of guy Paul was. He wanted everything he did to show other people what God was like. He knew that if he ran away, the jailer wouldn't think much of God, and neither would the other prisoners who had just been listening to them sing praises to God. So, Paul did the right thing . . . the hard thing, and stayed in the prison, even encouraging the other prisoners to stay, too. Because Paul behaved this way, the jailer wanted to know about God and he and his whole family became Christians!

It's not always easy to do the right thing. In fact, it's usually easier to do something else. But, doing the right thing, and not taking the easy way out is better in the long run.

Dad's Turn

Tell your son about a time when your crowd of friends was doing something you knew wasn't right, and you had to choose between doing the easy thing—going along with the crowd, or the hard thing—standing up for what you knew was right. What did you do? How did you feel about it afterwards? How did your friends feel about your choice?

Talk with your son about peer pressure and how there will be times when the crowd will want him to do something which he knows is not the right thing to do. Encourage him to be strong and do the right thing. Remind him that pleasing God, and obeying him will always be better in the long run.

A Verse to Remember

Honor the LORD and serve him wholeheartedly.
Joshua 24:14

Sailing to Disaster!

"Take me to Rome! I am a Roman citizen and I demand to be tried by Caesar instead of your little court!" Paul could be very insistent when he wanted to be. This time he was fighting for his life. He knew that he hadn't done anything wrong. There was no real reason for him to be in prison. He also knew that the Jewish leaders were going to have him killed just because of his faith in Christ. So, he had to get to Rome where he had a better chance of a fair trial.

"Get moving!" the guard cracked his whip to get the prisoners moving onto the prison ship. The men were chained together, so they couldn't move too quickly, but the guard didn't seem to care about that. "Move it!" the snap of the whip on one man's back made the prisoners hustle more quickly.

A couple of weeks into the journey toward Rome, a strong wind picked up and the sea waters got very choppy. "Storm coming!" the sailors shouted. Everyone jumped to their assigned jobs to prepare the ship for making it through the high winds and waves. Panic showed in the sailors' faces, "We're taking on water. Work you slaves, tie down the cargo! Do you want to sink?" The guards beat the slaves more than ever as they pushed them to work harder.

As the storm picked up and the ship took on water, the prisoners grabbed buckets and bailed as fast as their chains would let them. But, the ship sank lower and lower in the water. "Throw anything you can grab overboard! We've got to lighten her load!" the captain called. Day after day the sailors bailed water and fought the storm. They didn't even take time to eat!

"Calm down!" Paul shouted over the wind. "Stop and eat something. You've got to keep your strength up! It's going to be OK. God told me that the ship will sink, but we will all be saved. Trust him!" But, no one would listen to Paul, until the ship hit some rocks and was beaten to pieces by the wind and waves . . . but every person on board made it safely to shore . . . just as God said they would!

Based on Acts 27:13-44

Becoming a Man of God
A man of God doesn't panic.

Panicking is the easy thing to do in a crisis. All the sailors were panicked in this storm, even though they were experienced and knew what to do. Only Paul remained calm. That's because he wasn't depending on sailing experience or how well the ship was built to keep him calm and safe. He was depending on God. When everything seems to be going wrong and everything you normally depend on falls apart, what is left? God. And God is all you need.

What kinds of things make you very nervous and worried? Thunder storms? Ocean waves? Hearing your friends or family argue? Who can you trust to get you through these scary times?

Dad's Turn

Tell your son about a time when you were really frightened. How old were you? What was so scary about the situation? What did you do? How did it turn out? How do you usually handle your fears and worries?

Talk to your son about what kinds of things frighten him. How can you help him learn to work through these fears? Does he feel better when you pray together about them? Remind him of the ways God takes care of him every day. Encourage him to trust God to handle his fears now.

A Verse to Remember

Give all your worries and cares to God, for he cares about what happens to you.

1 Peter 5:7

Share a Bible Story Together